Knightly Memories

This is the first book-length study of the legacy and memory of the main military orders in Britain, the Templars and Knights of St. John. It provides a survey from the late 18th to the early 20th centuries using hitherto neglected sources and identifies areas for further research and analysis.

The volume first examines the historiography of the Orders, delving past the standard histories to examine their authors, readership, accessibility, advertisements and reviews. It then discusses the material memory of the Orders, from the Temple Church in London and St. John's Gate at Clerkenwell to archaeological discoveries and romanticised stained-glass depictions. Turning next to the revival and reinvention of the Order of St John after the loss of Malta in 1798 and the foundation of the British Order based at Clerkenwell, it unravels fact from fiction in the claims of continuity with the medieval knights made by the Masonic Knights Templars. For many, memory was shaped by popular fiction as well as history, so the final part considers various literary interpretations of the Orders' history.

This book will interest scholars and students of the Military Orders and Crusades, as well as general readers of the history of memory and reception.

Elizabeth Siberry is an independent scholar who has written books, chapters and many journal articles on the memory and legacy of the Crusades and military orders in Britain, including the volumes *The New Crusaders: Images of the Crusades* (2000) and *Tales of the Crusaders* (2021).

The Military Religious Orders: History, Sources, and Memory
Edited by Jochen Burgtorf and Nicholas Morton

The military religious orders were initially established in the twelfth century to care for and protect western pilgrims in the Holy Land. They later helped to defend the crusader states, participated in the Iberian Reconquista, and eventually played a significant role in warfare, charity, commerce, colonization, and cross-cultural encounters in Europe, the Mediterranean World, and even the New World. *The Military Religious Orders: History, Sources, and Memory* stimulates research on this fascinating phenomenon.

Knightly Memories

Remembering and Reinventing the
Military Orders in Britain

Elizabeth Siberry

Routledge
Taylor & Francis Group

LONDON AND NEW YORK

First published 2024
by Routledge
4 Park Square, Milton Park, Abingdon, Oxon OX14 4RN

and by Routledge
605 Third Avenue, New York, NY 10158

Routledge is an imprint of the Taylor & Francis Group, an informa business

British Library Cataloguing-in-Publication Data
A catalogue record for this book is available from the British Library

ISBN: 978-1-032-01118-9 (hbk)
ISBN: 978-1-032-01121-9 (pbk)
ISBN: 978-1-003-17723-4 (ebk)

DOI: 10.4324/9781003177234

Typeset in Times New Roman
by codeMantra

Contents

Figures

Acknowledgements

In writing this book, I have benefitted from access to a number of archives and libraries. I am most grateful for the assistance of the archivists of the Inner and Middle Temples in London; the Order of St. John in Clerkenwell; the British Association of the Catholic Sovereign Order of Malta, again in London; the Society of Antiquaries; Dorset Archives; the Worcestershire Masonic Museum and Yale University. In tracking down illustrations, I have also been helped by Chetham's Library in Manchester and the Royal Collection Trust.

Introduction

Much has been written about the medieval Military Orders in Britain, and, in particular, the Knights of St. John (or the Hospitallers) and the Templars.[1] The facts and chronology of their foundation, development, work and dissolution are well known. Key documents have been edited and detailed research has also been done on their finances, properties and related archaeology. There are material remains of both Orders throughout Britain, in churches and secular buildings such as barns and place names recall the history of long lost properties. We also have lists of members of the Orders and some of their personal histories and achievements, which were celebrated and, in some cases, invented by later generations.

More recently, there has been an increasing interest in the 'afterlife' of the Orders and attempts to revive them after the loss of Malta in 1798 and in the nineteenth century.[2] Most histories of the Orders now include a final chapter on this subject and the modern memory of the Military Orders in Britain and other countries was the subject of a recent volume in the *Engaging the Crusades* series.[3]

Histories of the Knights of St. John routinely follow the story through to the present day and the debate about the Templars and claims of their survival after the dissolution of the Order and death of the last Grand Master in 1314 continue to inspire a wealth of books and articles.[4] Peter Partner, who led the way with his 1981 book *The Murdered Magicians*, coined a term for this, namely, Templarism.[5]

This book, part of the Routledge series *The Military Religious Orders: History, Sources and Memory*, builds on these earlier publications and is the first book-length study of the legacy and memory of the Orders in Britain. As such, it provides a survey of the subject and identifies some avenues for further research and detailed analysis, highlighting a range of hitherto neglected sources. It might be described as a counterpart to books on the more developed subject, namely, the memory of the crusades[6] and it draws on a growing body of contextual research on medievalism, the history of memory, reception history and the history of material culture.[7] The timeframe covered are the late eighteenth, nineteenth and early twentieth centuries.

DOI: 10.4324/9781003177234-1

Chapter 1 will analyse what was available to read about the history of the Orders: who chose to write about them and why, from members of the Orders to historians of chivalry, authors of articles in journals and encyclopaedias and accounts of travellers to Rhodes and Malta. It will, however, consider more than the simple historiography. Library and book sale catalogues provide a useful indication of the availability of these works and other sources shed light on how they were received and interpreted. A key, and hitherto relatively unexplored source for this, will be the reviews published in a variety of periodicals and journals. They reflect not only the views of their authors but also the editorial stance of the 'host' publication and its expectations of its readers' knowledge of the subject, including their access to works published in French and German. An additional perspective is offered by comments in readers' diaries and letters and the popularity of engravings meant that histories were often illustrated, creating widely available images of the knights and key events in their history.

Two works – Abbe Vertot's *Historie des Chevaliers Hospitaliers*, first published in French in 1726, but available in numerous editions and translations thereafter and the lawyer Charles Greenstreet Addison's *History of the Templars*, published in 1842 – will be discussed in more detail as a window into readership and responses in this period.

My focus will be on the Templars and Knights of St. John, as the two major Orders with a British footprint. Some information would, however, also have been available about the Hospitals of St. Lazarus and St. Thomas of Acre in Britain and popular histories of chivalry and knighthood provided details of Orders established elsewhere in Europe and the Holy Land.[8]

Chapter 2 will then look at the way in which material remains have shaped the memory of the Orders. These range from medieval effigies in churches said to commemorate Knights of St. John or Templars to their round churches and in particular the Temple church in London. The Templars were succeeded by lawyers as occupants of this historic site and they drew links between the past and present in a variety of ways. The decoration and restoration of the Temple Church has been the subject of detailed study,[9] but little notice has been taken to date of services at key anniversaries, such as the 700th anniversary of its dedication by Patriarch Heraclius of Jerusalem in 1185 and the capture of Jerusalem in December 1917; the text of sermons preached on these occasions and their subsequent reporting. The chequered history of St. John's Gate and church at Clerkenwell in London also provided the backcloth to the revival of the Order of St. John in Britain. Elsewhere, the restoration of other churches and properties associated with the Orders in the nineteenth century created a visual image of knights of the Orders in, for example, stained glass. These reveal a variety of interpretations by different artists and designers and patrons or funders clearly took an active interest in the evocation of their property's medieval history. Archaeological excavations and discoveries, during church restorations, also stimulated interest in the history of the Orders and provoked some controversy.

Chapter 3 will turn from words and physical remains or images to the revival and reinvention of the orders in the nineteenth century. Some work has already been done on the early troubled years of the revived English langue and its subsequent reinvention as the Order of St. John of Jerusalem based at Clerkenwell, but archives at St. John's Gate and elsewhere shed fresh light on some of the individuals involved, their motivation and attitudes towards the Order. In parallel, some British catholics were created knights of the Sovereign Order of Malta and the British Association was established in 1875. The debate about the legality of the Protestant Order of St. John was aired not only in formal documents, but also in the newspapers and journals of the day and these sources have again hitherto been little explored. The decoration of the Order's headquarters and its assemblage of artefacts from its history, as well as the celebration of key anniversaries, were also important building blocks for the Order's future.

The attempts to revive the Templars are more complex and it can be difficult to disentangle facts from myth and invention. Nevertheless, there is a story to be told about attempts to revive the Templar Order in Britain, which involved a cast of colourful characters, such as the uncle of the poet Lord Alfred Tennyson. Templar history was also evoked by the Masonic Knights Templar, and other charitable organisations, such as the Good Templars. Brief reference will also be made to the use of the procedures and regalia of the medieval Orders by others, to establish their own, albeit short-lived, secular Orders.

The final chapter will look at the way in which members of the Orders and the institutions themselves have been portrayed in literature. The shadow cast by Sir Walter Scott is a long one and his treatment of the Orders and influence is a necessary starting point. It also provides evidence of the way in which stories evolved and were adapted for different audiences, from the formal theatre to pantomime and the penny dreadful. The actual history of the Order of St. John and the Templars, however, provided ample tales of dramatic sieges and trials and personal heroism in battle to inspire other poets and novelists, writing for both an adult and younger readership. As well as major writers such as Robert Browning, amateur poets found the history of the Orders a source of inspiration and a simple search in the British Library catalogue reveals a wealth of titles. Some of these were available in several editions and formats. Others were privately printed for circulation to friends, but they reveal an interest in the Orders and some knowledge of their past history. British readers also had access to French and German plays about the Orders such as Gotthold Lessing's *Nathan der Weise* in translation or indirectly through periodical reviews.

All these strands have therefore had a part to play in the way in which the Orders have been remembered in Britain.

Notes

1 See, for example, Jonathan Riley-Smith, *Hospitallers. The History of the Order of St John* (London, 1999); Helen Nicholson, *The Knights Templar* (London, 2010); Malcolm Barber, *The New Knighthood. A History of the Order of the Temple* (Cambridge, 1994).

2 See Riley-Smith, 'The Order of St. John in England, 1827–58' in *MO* 1, 121–412; Elizabeth Siberry, 'Victorian Perceptions of the Military Orders', *MO* 1, 365–72 and 'Images and Perception of the Military Orders in Nineteenth Century Britain', *Ordines Militares-Colloquia Torunensia Historica* 11 (2001), 197–209.

3 *The Modern Memory of the Military-Religious Orders*, ed. Rory MacLellan, *Engaging the Crusades*, vol. 7 (2022).

4 John Walker, 'From the Holy Grail and the Ark of the Covenant to Freemasonry and the Priory of Sion-An Introduction to the after History of the Templars' and Juliette Wood, 'The Myth of Secret Society or It's Not Just the Templars Involved in Absolutely Everything', *MO* 5, 449–60; Michael Haag, *The Templars. History and Myth* (London, 2008), pp. 238–83.

5 Peter Partner, *The Murdered Magicians. The Templars and Their Myth* (repr. Oxford, 1987).

6 See Mike Horswell, The Rise and Fall of British Crusader Medievalism, c.1825–1945 (Abingdon, 2018); Siberry, *The New Crusaders. Images of the Crusades in the 19th and Early 20th Centuries* (Aldershot, 2000) and *Tales of the Crusaders-Remembering the Crusades in Britain* (Abingdon, 2021).

7 See for example, Ika Willis, *Reception* (Abingdon, 2018); Louise D'Arcens, 'The Crusades and Medievalism', *Cambridge Companion to the Literature of the Crusades* (Cambridge, 2019), pp. 248–63; Kristin Skotti, 'The Dead, the Revived and the Recreated Pasts: "Structural Amnesia" in Representations of Crusade History', *Engaging the Crusades* 1 (2018), pp. 107–33.

8 See below, p. 5.

9 *The Temple Church in London. History, Architecture and Art*, ed. Robin Griffith-Jones and David Park (Woodbridge, 2017).

1 Knightly reading

Historiography, reading and reception

The history of the Knights of St. John and the Templars could be found in the seventeenth- and eighteenth-century histories of the crusades such as Thomas Fuller's *Historie of the Holy Warre* published in 1639.[1] They were also discussed in a number of popular general histories of orders of knighthood and chivalry such as Andrew Favine's *Theatre of Honour and Knighthood* published in 1623; Elias Ashmole's *The Institution, Laws and Ceremonies of the Most Noble Order of the* Garter from 1672; Hugh Clark's *History of Knighthood* published in 1784 and Susannah Dobson's *Historical Anecdotes of Heraldry and Chivalry* from 1795.[2] All these fed a growing interest in heraldry and genealogy and the history of the Military Orders was recorded as part of this story.

References in bibliographies and correspondence published in periodicals confirm that these works were consulted by later historians, but with the growth in publishing in the nineteenth century the history of the Military Orders was much more widely available. For example, it could be found in general histories of the crusades and Middle Ages, as well as dedicated monographs on the Knights of St. John and Templars. Readers would also have had access to articles in a range of popular encyclopaedias and some editions of primary sources, as well as the accounts of travellers to Rhodes and Malta. Memories were not only created by words. Many of these works were illustrated with scenes from the history of the Orders, such as the great siege of Malta in 1565 and portraits of individual knights and Grand Masters.

This chapter will look at a selection of such histories; explore the background of the authors and what inspired them to put pen to paper. Drawing on library catalogues, book sales and records of private reading to be found in letters and diaries, it will also consider the availability and popularity of such works and what they reveal about attitudes to the medieval military orders. These are all 'new sources', but there are other avenues of research still to be explored. Some histories appeared as monographs, others in series aimed at different categories of general reader and the choices made by publishers and the publication vehicle they selected as described in their own records is an aspect of historiography which remains to be examined.

DOI: 10.4324/9781003177234-2

It is not intended to provide a definitive historiography, but rather to highlight the diversity of publications and authors as reference points for the reception history of the Orders in this period. Two particular works will be discussed in more detail: Abbe Vertot's *Histoire des Chevaliers Hospitaliers* published first in 1726 and then in an English translation two years later and Charles Greenstreet Addison's *History of the Templars*, first published in 1842.

The existence of a book does not necessarily mean that it was read, but it would have become known outside the bookshop or library shelf through reviews and publishers' advertisements which appeared in a wide variety of popular periodicals and magazines. These would have reached a much wider audience than standard published histories and the editorial position of these publications reflected a range of religious and political perspectives, which, in turn, influenced their reviewers' attitude to the Military Orders. Often lengthy and detailed, such book reviews provided a platform for the, usually anonymous, author to set out his or her views on the Orders and, in so doing, display their own reading and knowledge of the subject. A variety of public and private libraries and other meeting places such as coffee houses also enabled access well beyond their subscriber base.

Periodicals also published articles on the history of the Orders, reflecting local and national archaeological and antiquarian research and discoveries. They also show that at least some British readers had access to and familiarity with works published outside Britain and in other European languages.

These sources, hitherto little explored by historians of the Orders, illustrate both the diversity of opinion and the way in which such views were informed and shaped. The boundary between history and literature was often blurred and a later chapter will therefore look at the evolving literary image of the knights, as a further piece of the reception picture.

The approach taken to the historiography will be chronological and start with the Knights of St. John, followed by the Templars, although of course some histories covered both. Chapter 2 will then discuss the history of the Temple church and the interest in the Order taken by members of the legal Inns of Court, some of whom wrote their own histories.

Knights of St. John or Hospitallers

Vertot's history

The French historian and ecclesiastic, Rene d'Aubert, known as Abbe de Vertot, was the author of several works of history, but the one relevant here is his four volume *Histoire des Chevaliers Hospitaliers*, published in Paris in 1726. A history of the Order by the knight Giacomo de Bosio had already been published in 1621, but the popularity of Vertot's work opens a new window into interest in the knights in Britain in the eighteenth and nineteenth centuries.

Controversial in its own time, being added to the Catholic church's Index list of prohibited books and denounced by the Order itself, there is evidence that it was widely available and read.[3]

Within ten years of publication, there were eight editions in four different countries and three languages. And further editions and translations, illustrated with engravings, were produced in the course of the eighteenth and nineteenth centuries. Its publishing history has been the subject of a detailed study by Robert Thake and this, coupled with evidence from other largely untapped sources such as library and book catalogues, letters and diaries, sheds important and fresh light on its popularity in Britain and consequential interest in the history of the Order.[4]

Some eighteenth-century readers

The first English edition of Vertot's work appeared in the summer of 1728 and was favourably reviewed in the journal *The Present State of the Republick of Letters* and advertised in newspapers and journals of the day.[5] Catalogues of book auctions in England between 1730 and 1800 analysed by Thake also show that Vertot could be found in the private libraries of not just antiquarians, but also politicians and members of the professional classes, from doctors to clerics and lawyers. These included the diplomat Sir Luke Schaub; the Archbishop of Armagh, Revd. Dr. William Newcome and the Bishops of Bristol and Bath and Wells.[6] And Edward Gibbon, who of course wrote about the crusades in his *Decline and Fall of the Roman Empire*, had a copy of Vertot in his library, although he rather dismissed his work as akin to a historical novel.[7]

Public or subscription library catalogues provide further evidence of its popularity, with some indications of actual reading and interest. Using modern databases of, for example, properties owned by the National Trust, one can see that both the French and English editions of Vertot could, and still can, be found in country house libraries across Britain. Those with surviving bookplates indicate that they formed part of the family library such as the copy with the bookplate of John Brownlow, Viscount Tyrconnel of Belton House, Lincolnshire.[8] And the catalogue of books owned by the Exeter book collector, Dr. Benjamin Heath, included the 1726 original French edition.[9] The architect and founder member of the Royal Academy (RA), William Chambers, was also given a copy of Vertot on a visit to Paris in 1784, which he subsequently sold to the RA, in whose library it remains.[10]

Vertot also had what might be described as a literary footprint. We know from his diary that the history was being read by the philosopher and novelist William Godwin in February 1799[11] and the novelist Henry Fielding was sufficiently familiar with the work to reference it as a source for the play *Elmerick or Justice Triumphant* – performed at the Theatre Royal in Drury Lane, London, in February 1740.[12]

These are records of ownership and interest without critical comment, but the correspondence between members of the eighteenth-century female London literary circle, known as the Bluestockings, shows that they both read and discussed Vertot. In May 1768, Catherine Talbot, whose stepfather Thomas Secker held high ecclesiastical office and encouraged her intellectual interests, wrote to her friend, the poet Elizabeth Carter, that she had just begun Vertot's *Chevaliers de Malte*, which she had borrowed from their friend Elizabeth Montagu[13] and it was recommended by the distinguished writer and lexicographer, Dr Samuel Johnson, to his friend the Revd. Astle in Ashbourne, Derbyshire.[14] A further measure of continued popularity was the competition between London and Edinburgh booksellers on pricing and further English editions were published in 1757, 1763, 1770, 1774 and 1775.[15]

Not all, however, agreed with such recommendations. In a letter in August 1748, Lord Chesterfield advised his son to inform himself about the history of the Military Orders because he might come across them on his travels, but he did not suggest Vertot's history because 'it is the least valuable of all his works and, moreover, too long for you to read'.[16] And, although the polymath Horace Walpole, who claimed a crusading ancestor, praised the history and had his own copy at his home Strawberry Hill, in Twickenham near London, his friend the Marquise du Deffand wrote in November 1770 that she had not been able to finish it and wished that the author had exercised his talents in another way.[17]

Nineteenth-century readers

The catalogues of nineteenth-century London booksellers such as Henry Bohn and William Mason provide continuing evidence of Vertot's popularity and one can therefore assume at least some interest in the history of the Order. In 1821 and 1841, both advertised a 1770 edition of the history and in 1848, Bohn had for sale two of the four-volume French editions and one of the 1728 English translation. In his 1841 catalogue, John Bohn advised that all Vertot's historical works deserve a careful reading because 'he is a first rate author'.[18]

The nineteenth century saw a significant increase in the number and variety of both private subscription and free public libraries throughout Britain and their printed catalogues and, where they survive, borrowing records are another indicator of reception and interest in the Orders. In London, Vertot could be found in the collection of the London Library founded in 1841, where it was borrowed by, among others, Colonel Maberley, a British army officer and later MP and the Prince Regent, later King George IV, acquired a copy of the 1726 French edition in 1815, which remains in the Royal Collection.[19] Vertot's work was also listed in the catalogues of libraries in the growing industrial centres of Britain such as The Athenaeum and Lyceum in Liverpool; Chetham's and the Portico Library in Manchester; the subscription library in Kingston upon Hull and the Library of the Writers to the Signet (a private society of Scottish solicitors) in Edinburgh.[20]

Readers could also turn for guidance on reading material to published lists of recommended works and these provide another indicator of interest in both the subject of the Orders and Vertot's history of the Knights of St. John. For example, it was among the 'approved authors' championed by the Revd. Henry Kett, a fellow of Trinity College Oxford, for the improvement of his young readers and it was also included in Daniel Appleton's *Library Manual* of 1852, which aimed to list the 'most important works in every department of knowledge in all modern languages'.[21] The historian of the crusades, Charles Mills, however, disagreed, describing Vertot, which he listed as a key source for Gibbon, as 'an amusing but superficial performance'.[22]

We rarely know how often the work was borrowed from libraries and actually read, but there is some evidence from letters and diaries suggesting a range of readership from poets to philosophers. Lord Byron listed Vertot among the history books which he had read and he visited Malta himself in August 1809 and May 1811, en route to and from the East.[23] And in 1824, Harriet Edgeworth, half sister of the novelist Maria Edgeworth, wrote to her aunt Harriet Beaufort about reading Vertot.[24] Sir Walter Scott also described it as a book which 'as it hovered between history and romance, was exceedingly dear to me' and he took his copy of the four-volume French edition with him when he travelled to Malta in 1830/1.[25]

Vertot himself even merited an entry in Charles Knight's *Penny Cyclopaedia* published in 1843. His verdict on the history of the Order, however, was mixed:

> Inferior in point of finish and picturesque energy to his earlier writings but infinitely more valuable on account of its originality. His access to authentic information rendered it valuable and might have done so to a greater extent had he possessed more the spirit of a historian and less that of a mere narrator.[26]

History and travel

Travellers to the sites associated with the Order could also read about its history in various publications.

Rhodes

Visitors to Rhodes would, for example, have been able to access the history of the knights through books such as the antiquarian and lawyer Cecil Torr's *Rhodes in Modern Times*, first published in 1881. He had criticisms of the histories produced by both Bosio and Vertot and argued, in rather a sweeping statement, that 'anything approaching an authentic history of the knights has yet to be written'.[27]

Some readers would also have had access to primary sources. The victorious defence of the island in 1480 was celebrated in an eyewitness account,

Descriptio obsidione Rhodie, by the Vice Chancellor of the Order, Guillaume Caoursin, which became a best seller, with several more editions before 1500, as well as translations into English, German, Italian and Danish.[28] The 1482/3 English translation by John Kaye was dedicated to King Edward IV.[29] Numerous copies of the various early editions have survived and, as an indication of continued interest, it was reprinted in a collection of works about the crusades published by Andrew Murray in 1870.[30] In 1926, it was also published, with an Introduction by the historian of the modern Order, Sir Edwin King, in advance of the pilgrimage to sites associated with its history. King noted:

> In all the long and glorious history of the Order of St. John of Jerusalem, adorned as it is by so many noble feats of arms, there is no episode which stirs the imagination as the Grand Master Peter d'Aubusson's successful defence of Rhodes in 1480.[31]

A copy of the first edition of Caoursin's work was also purchased for the St. John's Museum in Clerkenwell.

Inspired by Malta

Eighteenth-century British travellers, such as the antiquarian Sir Richard Colt Hoare and Scottish author Patrick Brydone, also visited Malta and wrote about the sites associated with the Order. Indeed Hoare had two copies of Vertot in his library at his home Stourhead, Wiltshire.[32]

Napoleon's capture of Malta in 1798 and the eviction of the knights, followed by the island's occupation by the British, created new interest in their history. The French Count Pierre Marie Louis de Boisgelin had become a member of the Order in 1782 and lived in Malta until 1793, before ultimately settling in Britain. In London in 1804, he published a detailed two-volume history of island and the Order including 'a particular account of the events which preceded and attended its capture by the French and Conquest by the English'. He lamented the fate of both the island and its former knightly occupants:

> It appears therefore extraordinary that an Order ever distinguished for its piety, military exploits and wise form of government-an order which had hitherto triumphed even in the midst of misfortunes-should cease to exist and no kind pen, no friendly hand, be found to rescue it from oblivion.

Keen to record the Order's noble past, Boisgelin also provided a list of published histories, citing Vertot as 'amongst the most useful' and gave a detailed account of its statutes, finances and military successes.[33]

Scott asked for a copy of Boisgelin's book to be sent to him as he travelled to Malta, but the author of a review in the *Edinburgh Review* in 1805 was unimpressed and described the book as 'destitute of merit' preferring Vertot:

> The only original thing in the book, and almost the only amusing one, is the author's zeal for his Order, and his anxiety that the island should be restored to it. Is it possible that any man of common sense should fail to see, that the institution has already outlived its utility, and is daily becoming ridiculous? It would not be more absurd, to give an island to a lodge of Freemasons, than to such a corporation as the Knights of Malta.[34]

There has been some debate about the identity of this reviewer. Scott believed that it was Henry, Lord Brougham, a regular contributor to the *Review,* but it has also been attributed to John Stoddart, King's Advocate in Malta from 1803–7 and later editor of *The Times.*[35]

Malta was a regular stop for cruises run by the Peninsular and Oriental Company (P&O) and members of the army and navy both served there and visited en route back from service in India or elsewhere in the Mediterranean. One such, Captain James William Bryans, a retired lieutenant of the Bombay army, became interested in the history of the knights, and wrote of his experiences in an article for *Colburn's United Service Magazine.* He was taken by a local guide, whose father had been a member of the Order, to see the memorials in the cathedral of St. John in Valletta and wrote that he 'cast a lingering and cherished thought on the wonderful and unparalleled achievements of the Knights of St. John of Jerusalem'. Bryans went on to become a member of the English Order then struggling for recognition and expressed a hope that this 'band of spirited and noble Englishmen... may find an echo in the breast of many who are able to give it that support which it so deservedly requires'.[36] Claudius Shaw, a retired Colonel, who had served in Malta and became a knight of St. John, similarly linked the Order's past and present:

> Even at the present day, after existing for nearly 800 years without a broken link in the chain, kings, noblemen and gentleman of the highest stations, are proud of being admitted to join its ranks.[37]

Another visitor, the lawyer Charles Addison, who began his 1835 journey to Damascus and Palmyra at Malta, noted:

> The beautiful churches of Malta, the gorgeous cathedral with its interesting associations, the palace of the Grand Master, the library, and the handsome palaces of the knights, converted into clubs, mess-rooms and barracks, well merit attention; and the inspection of the fortifications...necessarily detain the traveller some days at this interesting spot.[38]

A steady stream of British visitors also visited Malta's warmer climes for their health. Many would have seen the physical legacy of the Order in buildings such as the Castle of St. Elmo, the former residence of the Grand Master and the magnificent tombs and memorial tablets at St. John's cathedral. They would also have read about its history in guidebooks and in particular the events of the great siege of 1565.[39]

One popular *Guide to Malta and Gozo*, first published in 1838, but thereafter in numerous editions, was written by the Anglican missionary George Percy Badger. He described Malta as 'the bulwark of Christendom' and hailed the benefits of British rule, occupying:

> Under the benign and all powerful flag of Great Britain, a prouder attitude than even during the most renowned days of her chivalrous story, under the sovereignty of the Knights of St. John of Jerusalem.

Badger provided his readers with a history of the Order up to the French occupation and the buildings which it occupied, including the English Auberge 'at present occupied by the officers of the British garrison'.[40]

There were souvenirs for sale such as papier mache figures of knights and one, now in the Royal Collection, was a memento from Prince Albert Edward's (later King Edward VII) visit to Malta in 1861.[41] Other examples are on display in the Museum of St. John in Clerkenwell.[42] Engravings of portraits of key figures such as the Grand Masters at the sieges of Rhodes and Malta were available for purchase and there were editions of engravings of the series of eight paintings depicting the 1565 siege, by the Italian artist Matteo Perez d'Aleccio.[43] The Tower of London also has on display a cannon from Malta, which was described and illustrated in London guides.[44]

But not all were respectful of the Order's history. In his *Notes of a Journey from Cornhill to Grand Cairo* published in 1846, William Thackeray, who visited Malta in 1844, declared:

> What faith, endurance, genius and generosity; what pride, hatred, ambition and savage lust of blood were raised together for their guardianship.[45]

Like many visitors he was struck by the elaborate memorials to knights in St. John's cathedral, noting that the floor:

> Is paved over with sprawling heraldic devices of the dead gentlemen of the dead Order; as if in the next world they expected to take rank in conformity with their pedigrees and would be marshalled into heaven according to their orders of precedence.[46]

Histories of the order

The fate of the Order after 1798; the British occupation of Malta, which became a crown colony in 1814 and attempts to revive the English langue culminating, as will be discussed in Chapter 3, in the re-establishment of the Order of St. John of Jerusalem based at Clerkenwell, provided the stimulus for a variety of other nineteenth-century histories by a diverse group of authors.

In 1830, Scott's Edinburgh publisher, Archibald Constable, published Alexander Sutherland's two volume *The Achievements of the Knights of Malta*. It appeared as number 53 (of 80) in the series entitled *Miscellany of original and selected publications in various departments of Literature, Science and Arts*, priced at one shilling. The dedication to Tsar Nicholas of Russia, 'under whose imperial protection the banner of that ancient and illustrious order is still unfurled' suggests what inspired the choice of subject and Sutherland noted that 'scarcely 30 years have elapsed since foreign violence and political craft, combined with their own degeneracy, deprived the knights of Malta of their independence', although he chose to finish his history with the election of Grand Master Pierre D'Aubusson in 1476. His sources included not only Vertot, but also Boisgelin and Henry Stebbing's 1825 *History of Chivalry and the Crusades*, which had been an earlier volume in the Constable series. As an indicator of possible readership, Sutherland's history could be found on the shelves of libraries such as the free Central Lending Library in Newcastle, which was the first subscription library in England and the Liverpool Lyceum. It was also quoted as the source by a number of authors.[47]

Those involved in the controversial attempts to revive the English langue in the mid-nineteenth century were understandably keen to remind both supporters and critics of the Order's noble history. Thus, Richard Broun, the Grand Secretary of the langue from 1837 until his death in 1858, produced his *Synoptical Sketch of the Illustrious and Sovereign Order of Knights Hospitallers of St. John of Jerusalem and of the Venerable Langue of England* for distribution to fellow members. And, in 1850, a history of the 1565 siege of Malta was published by 'a knight of the renovated Order'. He wrote that the possessions of the Order had been 'disgracefully pillaged', but praised the distinguished service of some English knights during the Ottoman siege. He had clearly visited the island and described the way in which the defeat of the Turks had been celebrated up to 1798:

> On the 8th of September while the knights had dominion over the stoned rock at Malta, a high festival was celebrated in memory of the raising of the siege on that day. In the magnificent church of St. John, crowded with the splendid trophies and insignia of the order…a knight clothed in complete mail carried the great standard of St. John to the high altar, and there displayed its victorious folds amid salvoes of artillery and bursts of martial music.[48]

After the break with the Sovereign Order in 1858, those working to re-establish and garner support for the Order in Britain, such as Richard Woof, of whom more later, similarly drew on its past to underpin and justify their activities.[49]

John Taaffe approached the subject from a different perspective, as a member of the catholic Sovereign Order. His four volume history published in 1852 may also have been inspired by a visit to Malta in 1848. A colourful character from a family in Co. Louth in Ireland which had links with the medieval military orders, he had been part of the Pisan circle of the poets Shelley and Byron in the 1820s and was the author of the first English commentary on Dante.[50] Taaffe also wrote two poems-*Padilla* and *Adelais*-set against the background of the crusades; the latter including a list of English knights 'to the glory of our most illustrious families'. Taaffe's history was reviewed in periodicals such as the *Athenaeum* and *Spectator* and quoted by other historians of the Order.[51] He also advocated the establishment of a permanent base for the Order in the Middle East under the protection of the Sultan of Turkey.[52]

Major General Whitworth Porter of the Royal Engineers, who published a history of the Knights of Malta in 1858, was a very different historian. His work, inspired by postings to Malta after service in the Crimean War and between 1870 and 1874, ran to over 700 pages and was the fruit of research in the archives of Malta. A later edition of 1883 was dedicated to his son Reginald, also an army officer, who was buried in Malta 'amid the dust of so many who, like him, fell in the sacred course of duty'. Porter noted that 'the encroachments of the infidel are no longer dreaded in Europe' and thereby the need for the Order itself. Nevertheless, the name and deeds of the Hospitallers deserved to be remembered:

> The days of chivalry are at an end; but the heart still throbs, and the pulse beats high, as we trace its career, like a meteor's flash, dazzling the page of history.[53]

After his retirement, Porter became involved in the Order of St. John's charitable work and was almoner of the English langue in the 1860s.[54]

A review of Porter's later edition in the Edinburgh based *Blackwood's* magazine argued that the history of the Order appealed to many different categories of reader:

> The subject, indeed, sparkles with many facets of interest. The medical man finds light thrown upon the early history of hospitals; the soldier reads...the animated narrative of the sieges of Rhodes and Malta...and the politician is interested in a constitution alien to any other in the world's history-the autocratic authority of a military chieftain tempered by the democratic equality of the convent.

The review's author, however, expressed concern that the historical artefacts of the Order were not being cared for as they deserved under British custo-dianship.[55] And, as will be discussed later in Chapter 3, Whitworth Porter's work also came under criticism from supporters of the catholic British Asso-ciation of the Sovereign Order of Malta.[56]

In 1869, Robert Bigsby, a former Registrar and Secretary of the Eng-lish langue, published his *Memoir of the Illustrious and Sovereign Order of St. John of Jerusalem from the capitulation of Malta in 1798 to the present period*. He also included a biographical roll of living and deceased members of English langue.[57] And in 1879, the Revd. Frederick Woodhouse, Rector of St. Mary's Hulme, Manchester, chronicled the Order's history in his *Military Religious Orders*, part of a series under the auspices of the Society for the Promotion of Christian Knowledge.[58]

Encyclopaedias and compilations

Articles drawing on the various histories also appeared in encyclopaedias such as the *Encyclopaedia Britannica* and *Chambers* and more popular ver-sions like the *Penny Cyclopaedia for the Diffusion of Useful Knowledge* and *Ebenezer Brewer's Dictionary of Phrase and Fable*. While these tended to be a synthesis of existing material, the bibliographies provided for further reading indicate a familiarity not only with histories in English, but also the works of Italian, German and French historians. For example, articles published in the 1886 edition of the *Encyclopaedia Britannica* and 1904 edi-tion of *Chambers* referenced Vertot, seventeenth-century histories in Italian by Bosio and Bartolomeo dal Pozzo and Delaville Le Roulx's cartulary, of which more below.[59]

Publication of primary sources

Those interested in the history of the Order could also access primary sources. A stay in Malta for his health in 1838–9 inspired the Revd. Lambert Larking, an enthusiastic antiquarian whose discoveries had included the heart shrine of the crusader Sir Roger Leybourne, to edit the 1338 report of Prior of the Order in England, Philip de Thame, which was published by the Camden Society in 1857. The Introduction, written by the historian John Mitchell Kemble, pre-sumed 'every educated Englishman to be well acquainted with the theory and the place in history of the Order' because:

> the influence of these great bodies was felt for centuries in every part of the world…it behoves the student of history to keep his eye steadily fixed upon their fortunes.[60]

The edition was given a lengthy review in *The Times* in May that year and described therein as:

> One of the most important documents for the history of culture that has for many years been brought to light. We are enabled to see the Hospitallers via an entirely new relation, not as in their half barrack half camp in Syria, or escorting trains of pilgrims to the banks of the Jordan, nor waging war against piratical Saracens; but as landlords and men of business, managing their estates with a shrewd eye to their own interests as well as those of Christendom...The world has now outgrown the necessity of such institutions as the Military Orders, but the time was when they had work to do and did it well. The influence they exerted lasted for centuries; and for an insight into the machinery by which that influence was sustained few historical documents will be found more useful than this 'books of accounts' which we have been reviewing.[61]

The *Gentleman's Magazine* also praised Larkin's work for shedding a new light on the history of the Order and providing valuable information for the research of the historian, genealogist and topographer.[62] This again suggests a wider circle of interest and readership.

William Winthrop, the American Consul General in Malta from 1834 until his death in 1869 and a Knight Commander of the Order, also made use of the Valletta archives, publishing a series of documents relating to the history of the Order in *Notes and Queries*, which, in turn, prompted follow up queries and correspondence. In addition, he provided a list of English, Irish and Scottish knights[63] and other articles in the *Gentleman's Magazine* discussed the family history of individual knights.[64]

The four volume Cartulary of the Order, published by the French historian and member of the Sovereign Order, Joseph Delaville Le Roulx, in Paris between 1894 and 1906 was the subject of detailed reviews in the *English Historical Review* between 1896 and 1902, by the Oxford historian Lucy Toulmin-Smith.[65] She had visited Malta in 1881, where she found both Delaville Le Roulx and the chaplain of the Order of St. John, William Bedford, working in the archives. In her letter from Valletta, published in *The Academy* in April 1881, Toulmin-Smith described the wealth of manuscripts about the history of the Order to be found in Malta, but also the conservation challenges faced by those responsible for their care, such as insect infestation:

> No one who saw a wild beast such as I caught a few days ago in one of the knights' registers in the archives here (where, however, they are comparatively rare)-nearly an inch long, horny with mandibles and many legs-will wonder at the mischief done by them in this warm and dusty climate, where insect life thrives lustily.[66]

Regional studies

Those living in sites across Britain associated with the Order also published articles in archaeological and regional history journals. For example, the Revd. Thomas Hugo, a keen antiquarian, chaplain of the Order and the reputed founder of the London and Middlesex Archaeological Society, wrote about the Order's holdings at Harefield Middlesex; the Preceptory at Mynchin Buckland in Somerset and the Commandery at Eagle in Lincolnshire.[67] Another clergyman, Revd. Shimfield of Wendy in Cambridgeshire, spoke to the Cambridge Antiquarian Society about the Preceptory of nearby Shengay[68] and in Oxfordshire, the Revd. C.J. Bowden wrote about the Hospitallers in his county.[69] Their footnotes illustrate the significance of Larking's work and the inspiration it provided for further documentary research and archaeological excavation.

The modern Order of St. John

The developments in the Order and its charitable work, particularly the foundation of the St. John Ambulance Association in 1878, left a gap in published histories and two officers, Richard Holbeche, Librarian from 1901, and William Bedford, chaplain to the Order, published their expanded history in 1902.[70] There was also a history of the Order by another officer, Henry Fincham, who was the first curator of the Order's Library and Museum, and he and others produced a series of pamphlets about aspects of the Order's history.[71]

First World War

The role played by the Order during the First World War encouraged more writers to pay tribute and emphasise the continuity between its modern work and its historical foundations. Writers such as the historian and novelist Eva Tenison, whose naval officer brother had been killed in 1916, took the story up to the end of the First World War and the role of the Order in that conflict and the Preface, by Field Marshal Sir Evelyn Wood, noted:

> Long dead but ever living heroes are the invisible leaders whose exploits, sacrifices and achievements spur us into action and awake in us a spirit of honourable emulation[72]

And in 1918, Rose Georgina Kingsley, the eldest child of the cleric and author Charles Kingsley, published *The Order of St. John of Jerusalem Past and Present*, noting that she wrote as 'news comes that Jerusalem, after 730 years is today safe in the hands of British, French, Italian and Indian troops'. The events referred to were of course the loss of Jerusalem to Saladin in 1187 and the 1917 capture of Jerusalem by the army under General Allenby.[73] The official history of the Order, however, fell to its Librarian, Colonel Sir Edwin King in 1924. In his Preface, he paid tribute to Vertot as 'one great historian' of the Order, noting that his own aim was 'to depict the part that Englishmen have played in it throughout the ages, and its history in our own land'. The second edition, published in 1934, covered the Order's activities across the British Empire and he also wrote about the history of the knights in the Holy Land (1931); a study of their seals (1932); the 1926 pilgrimage and the Order's rules, statutes and customs (1935).[74]

Tales of heroism

The motivation for the history published in 1858 by Augusta Drane was rather different. The daughter of an East India merchant, Drane taught in a school in London and in 1852, having converted to Catholicism, became a nun. She published lives of several saints and chose the subject of the Knights of St. John, coupled with the battle of Lepanto and Siege of Vienna, to provide 'a picture of events so memorable in the annals of the world'. Declaring the secular powers too much engaged in their rivalries and selfish preoccupations, she lauded the faith and courage of the knights as 'dutiful sons of the holy church':

> They confronted single-handed the enormous hosts of the infidels in their descents upon Europe, arrested their triumphant march towards the West, retreated from one position only to rally in another, and renew a contest which in appearance was hopeless; and at length, when all seemed lost, by sheer fortitude and perseverance they baffled and beat back the barbarian invader in the very pride of his strength, so that he never dared to approach their stronghold again.

And in this heroic struggle, she believed that they fought as the Pope's militia.[75] The basic chronology and key events of the Order's history were therefore available in a variety of publications and, with the re-establishment of the Order of St. John of Jerusalem in Britain, there was an understandable desire to record and remember its past as a foundation and inspiration for its future work and growing reputation.

The Templars

The nineteenth-century historiography of the Order of the Temple is more complicated and colourful and it can often be difficult to disentangle the myth making from straightforward history. A number of histories of the Order were, however, published in Britain and interested readers would also have been able to access and read editions of sources and histories in French and German.

As will be discussed in the next chapter, the history, trial and fate of the Templars and the Temple church itself inspired several later legal occupants of the Middle and Inner Temple to record the history of their medieval predecessors. Others involved in attempts to recreate the Order, such as James Burnes, also took up their pens.

One popular history of the Order by Charles Addison, a barrister and member of the Inner Temple in London, was published in 1842 and its reception, evidenced by a variety of sources, offers a window into knowledge of and attitudes towards the Templars at this time. Published catalogues show that Addison's history could be found in a number of British libraries[76] and the future Prime Minister, William Gladstone, recorded in his diary that he had read Addison's history of the Temple church and visited it on several occasions in 1842/3.[77] Addison's history was also reviewed in a range of periodicals, illustrating the diversity of views about the Templars and the different audiences considered likely to be interested in their story.

The conservative *Edinburgh Review* discussed Addison's work in a lengthy article entitled 'Knights Templars-Soldiers, Monks, Heretics', that also covered Joseph Francois Michaud's history of the crusades; Francois Raynouard's *Monuments Historiques relatifs a la condamnation des chevaliers du Temple*, published in Paris in 1813 and Pierre du Puy's *Histoire de la Condamnation des Templiers*, published in Brussels in 1751. The reviewer noted the 'drawn battle between their champions, apologists and foes' and the intrinsic interest of the subject and its individual stories:

> None transcend in dramatic interest the story of the Militia Christi, who for 200 years dominated the imagination of Christendom as the ideal soldiery of God, to close their career in ignominy, torture and death, as apostates for the religion whose cause they had for two centuries vindicated with their blood.[78]

He added that in the Order's history 'the ideal and the actual, purpose and practice, confront each other in sharpest antagonism'. The discussion of the Templars' trial cited other works by French and German writers, such as Jules Michelet and Joseph von Hammer Purgstall, and again highlighted the fate and suffering of those individuals, who were condemned to death, describing them as 'earth's noblest heroes'.[79] This was therefore much more than a simple review of books on the subject and reflected wider attitudes and quite extensive reading.

The more radical *Eclectic Review* welcomed Addison's history as an opportunity to set out the historical facts:

> Peculiar in their character, their usages, their duties, the knights templar have been presented in every strange and contradictory light…Now it must be obvious to every reader that such conflicting opinions arise from imperfect knowledge, and that a clearer view can be obtained only by tracing the progress of this formidable and valiant order, from the period of its foundation to that of its sudden and forcible suppression.

The reviewer concluded by criticising the church's legal process:

> Whenever the church has sought to wield the temporal sword, its character has become utterly changed; for whether the church court has been presided over by a pope or a consistory, an archbishop or a synod, its proceedings have ever been distinguished by a contempt for human rights, and a recklessness of human suffering, far beyond what the annals of the worst civil tribunals can show.[80]

In a two part review in the influential weekly literary journal, the *Athenaeum*, Hannah Lawrance, who had written elsewhere about the sources for the history of the crusades, noted both the interest in the subject and the gap that Addison's work filled:

> Among the many singular institutions of the Middle Ages, there are few more interesting than those half monastic, half military associations, which were formed for the purpose of checking the power of the Saracens…The history of the Hospitallers has been often written; but for the history of the Templars we have, until lately, been compelled to refer to the general history of the crusades…the volume before us therefore has appropriately fallen into the hands of a resident on the very spot where the chief house of the Templars in England stood.[81]

The perceived interest in the subject is also reflected in a review in a rather different publication, *The Court Magazine and Monthly Critic and Lady's Magazine*, which advised its readers that the work 'is a valuable library addition'. Another edition of the magazine gave an account of the restoration of the Temple church.[82]

The attempts to revive the Order of the Temple will be discussed in Chapter 3, but Addison's history continued to be drawn on as a source for the history of the Order by those who wished to argue its continuity from past to present. For example, an American edition of Addison, published by the Masonic Publishing Company of New York in 1873, expanded his original text citing Vertot, Michaud, Taaffe, Woof and many others, thus 'affording a complete history of Masonic knighthood from the origin of the Orders to the present time'.[83]

Addison wrote as a lawyer interested in the history of the Order and the Temple church, but other historians were motivated by a specific desire to defend the Order's reputation. In 1846, Thomas Keightley, also the author of a popular history of the crusades (1833–4), published *Secret Societies of the Middle Ages*. This also covered the Assassins and the Secret Tribunals of Westphalia, but most of the text was about the Templars and a defence of the charges laid against them, both at the time of their trial and by subsequent historians. Keightley explained his choice of title:

> To add one more to the number of their defenders…and to show how absurd and frivolous were the charges against them, are the objects of the present writer, who, though he is persuaded, and hopes to prove, that they held no secret doctrine, yet places them among the Secret Societies of the Middle Ages, because it is by many confidently maintained that they were such.[84]

In 1865, Anthony O'Neal Haye, editor of the *Scottish Freemason's Magazine*, also published a defence of the Templars, entitled *The Persecution of the Knights Templar*. He described it as 'a labour of love' and it followed a series of articles on the Order's history published in the *Freemasons Magazine and Masonic Mirror*.[85] Reviews in a variety of other periodicals, however, suggest that it attracted some more general interest.

The weekly *Saturday Review of Politics, Literature, Science and Art* was both critical of the absence of references and his partisan approach. It complimented Haye, as a Scotsman writing in Edinburgh, however, 'for a vigorous denunciation of the historical errors into which so many people have been led by the medieval romances of Sir Walter Scott'. The *Spectator* was slightly more positive, judging the story 'well and plainly' told, although it added little to 'our knowledge of the subject'. It even reached the pages of *The United Presbyterian Magazine*, whose reviewer approached the subject from a different perspective, suggesting its interest lay in the Templars' 'residence in the neighbourhood of Zion's sanctuary' and lamenting 'how miserably do modern representatives maintain the spirit of their predecessors'.[86] This all suggests a range of readers and commentators, who could take from the history of the Order evidence to suit their particular interest and perspective.

Documents: rule of the Templars

Some would also have had access to the text of the Rule of the Templars through Andrew Favine's chivalric compendium, *The Theatre of Honour and Knighthood*.

Favine, a Parisian lawyer, first published his detailed history of chivalry in Paris in 1620, but in 1623 it appeared in an English translation by the London publisher William Jaggard, who had printed Shakespeare's First Folio in the same year. Favine's work described the Orders of chivalry in the various European countries and he devoted the ninth book to the Holy Land and the history of the Military Orders, concluding with the text of the Templar Order, based on a manuscript in the Bibliotheque Nationale.[87] Walter Scott certainly had a copy of Favine's work in his library at Abbotsford and used it as a source for his novel *Ivanhoe*.[88] It was also mentioned as a source in Henry Stebbing's 1825 *History of Chivalry* and could be found in a number of public and private library catalogues of the period.[89]

References in articles and bibliographies suggest that there were other editions of the Rule consulted by interested historians of the Templars. A 1794 German translation of the Rule by the scholar and theologian Friedrich Munter was cited as a source by the lawyer and antiquarian Weston Styleman Walford, in an 1845 article about the Temple church[90] and the authorities listed in the *Encyclopaedia Britannica* included not only Henri de Curzon's *La Regle du Temple*, published in Paris in 1886, but also an earlier edition by Charles-Hippolyte Maillard de Chambure from 1840. In addition, in 1895, the catholic *Dublin Review* published a review of works about the fall of the Templars, which included Curzon's edition of the Rule.[91]

Lectures

The Templars were also discussed in a number of public lectures. In 1885, the historian James Anthony Froude, Regius Professor of History at Oxford, who is better known for his histories of the early modern period, was invited to give a lecture at the Edinburgh Philosophical Society. Having visited the Temple church in London, he decided to speak about the Templars and his essay of some 60 pages was subsequently published in 1892.[92] Froude noted the way in which the novels of Scott had coloured popular images of the knights, but he argued that he had chosen his subject because it illustrated some of the challenges of the use and value of historical evidence and belief. Concluding his history with the trial and dissolution of the Templars, Froude suggested that it might strike a chord with his Scottish audience:

> You in Scotland found no great reason to love bishops, and the history of the Templars does not increase our affection for them.[93]

Chambers' *Encyclopaedia* dismissed Froude's lectures as 'interesting but superficial', but the *Saturday Review* concluded:

> He has on the whole so handled it as to promote a sounder knowledge of one of the strangest episodes of medieval history.[94]

Froude's lectures would also have reached a wider audience through their publication in the monthly periodical *Good Words*, which had a circulation of over 100,000.[95]

There was also local antiquarian interest in Templar history. For example, the Revd. John Kendrick spoke to the Yorkshire Philosophical Society 'On the Rise and Suppression of the Templars in Yorkshire' in 1865;[96] John Crawford Hodgson, the author of a history of Northumberland, spoke to the Society of Antiquaries in Newcastle about the Temple Thornton farm accounts in 1895[97] and the Revd. Bentley, vicar of Bosbury in Herefordshire, whose church had two memorial slabs said to commemorate members of the Order, researched its preceptory there.[98]

There was a particular interest in the Templars in Scotland, with the popular, albeit spurious, claims that the last Templars had found refuge there. The Edinburgh lawyer, antiquarian and friend of Walter Scott, James Maidment, published two works of *Templaria* about the Order's Scottish possessions with relevant documents.[99] The knights were also the subject of articles in the *Aberdeen Journal, Scottish Review, Transactions of the Hawick Archaeological Society* and *Scottish Historical Review.*[100] The ruins of Templar buildings near the village of Temple in Midlothian inspired the Revd. Alfred Coutts to publish a short history of the Order[101] and Edinburgh, as the most important publishing centre outside London, was, of course, both the place of publication of Scott's novels and the histories of Sutherland and Haye already mentioned.

Lectures given outside Britain such as 'The Downfall of the Templars' by German historian Ignaz von Dollinger, also found publishers and translators for a British audience. It was among the *Addresses in historical and literary subjects* published by John Murray, translated into English, in 1894 and would, for example, have been available to members of the subscription Manchester Portico Library, which included among its members prominent local industrialists and the novelist Elizabeth Gaskell.[102]

Foreign language publications

As already noted, reviewers drew on histories published in other European languages and one example of this was a review article about the Templars, which appeared in *Eclectic Review* in July 1857. Its author argued that the subject was 'still so little known to the majority of English readers' and therefore called attention to histories published in Paris, Amsterdam and Lisbon. He concluded that the Templars:

> must always furnish a subject worthy of study and of interest to those who seek to discover the motives, or the characteristic exhibitions of the feelings, which actuate society.[103]

And in 1829, the *Foreign Quarterly Review* devoted a lengthy article to a history of the Order published by the young German historian Ferdinand

Wilcke.[104] Writing ten years after the publication of Scott's *Ivanhoe*, the reviewer argued that, while the Waverley novels had 'done some mischief from a historical point of view', they had begun to wean 'the public mind from the wretched trash in which it had previously been feeding' and welcomed signs that history was beginning to 'engage more attention and form a more prominent branch of study and literary education' in Britain, with publications such as Constable's *Miscellanies*. He (or she) did not think much of Wilcke's historical analysis and criticised his inability to distinguish between history and romance.[105] The same issue of the *Review* discussed the account of the Templars in Sismondi's mammoth *History of France*, published between 1818 and 1841.[106]

Wilcke was also one of the authorities cited by Thomas Keightley in his *Secret Societies* and another French history of the Templars, Philippe Grouvelle's *Mémoires historique sur les Templiers*, published in Paris in 1805, appeared in the very different collections of the antiquarian Francis Douce and the London physician James Franck.[107] The lawyer James Mackintosh also noted in his diary that he had been reading the history of the Templars by Grouvelle[108] and, like Vertot, it could be found on the shelves of the Kingston upon Hull subscription library.[109]

Conclusion

There was therefore no shortage of material to read and consult for those interested in the history of the military orders in Britain, representing a variety of views and by a range of authors. Such works could be found on the shelves of the growing number of free public and subscription libraries and reviews, diaries, letters and footnotes provide new evidence that such works were read and sparked debate about the history and fate of both the Hospitallers and Templars. Articles and reviews in periodicals offered different perspectives on the subject and would also have informed readers about books published elsewhere in Europe. In addition, those interested in the Orders were able to access a limited range of primary sources and one can identify the beginnings of local and regional studies of their lands and buildings.

Certain themes can be traced through the historiography of the Knights of St. John and the Templars. For the former, visits to Rhodes and Malta, the latter of course a British crown colony from 1814, inspired a study of the great sieges and achievements of knights who combined military prowess in a noble cause with care for the sick. Moreover, the articulation of historical continuity underpinned the attempt, ultimately successful but at the time controversial, to revive the English langue and the Order's charitable work. Catholic British members of the Sovereign Order of Malta similarly took pride in the Order's history. The motivation for Templar historiography was rather different. The dramatic fall of the Order and fate of its members encouraged historians (and lawyers) to analyse the material available and consider the accuracy of the charges levied at them and the motives of their accusers. For some Protestant writers and apologists, Templar history was simply another example of the failings of the medieval church and papacy. The linkage made between the Templars and freemasonry was a further spur to study and publish the history of their alleged predecessors. A review of knightly reading therefore provides more than just an analysis of individual publications. It sheds light on attitudes towards the Military Orders in this period and indeed the crusading movement as a whole.

Notes

1   Maclellan, 'Memories of the Military Orders in Britain in the Seventeenth and Eighteenth Centuries' in *The Modern Memory of the Military-Religious Orders*, pp. 4–21.
2   For Favine, see above, pp. 21–2. Hugh Clark wrote a popular introduction to heraldry as well as his *Concise History of Knighthood, Containing the Religious and Military Orders which have been Instituted in Europe* (London, 1784). For Ashmole, see Maclellan, pp. 8–11. Susannah Dobson, *Historical Anecdotes of Heraldry and Chivalry* (Worcester, 1795), pp. 128–72, was better known as a translator of Sainte Palaye's *Memoires sur l'ancienne chevalerie*, a key chivalric text.
3   See William Zammit, 'Vertot's Histoire des Chevaliers de Malte. Its Prohibition in the Context of Hospitaller Historiographical Practices', *Entre Deus e Rei. O mundo des Ordens Militares* (2018), 107–36 and Paul G. Pisani, 'Adaptations in Hospitaller Historiography. An Overview', *Symposia Melitensia* 8 (2012), 49–62.
4   Robert Thake, *A Publishing History of a Prohibited Best-Seller* (Delaware, 2016).
5   Ibid., pp. 146–56.
6   Ibid., pp. 329–36.
7   Geoffrey Keynes, *The Library of Edward Gibbon* (Dorchester, 1980).
8   National Trust Collections. www.nationaltrustcollections.org.uk, accessed 14 April 2023.
9   *A Catalogue of Books in the Various Branches of Literature Which Lately Formed the Library of a Distinguished Collector Dr. Heath* (London, 1810), p. 176.
10   www.royalacademy.org.uk, accessed 14 April 2023.
11   http://godwindiary.bodleian.ox.ac.uk, accessed 14 April 2023.
12   *Contributions to the Champion and Related Writings by Henry Fielding* ed. W.B. Coley (Oxford, 2003) p. 203.
13   Letter dated 31 May 1768. See UK Reading Experience Database. https://www.open.ac.uk/Arts/reading>UK, accessed 14 April 2023. History was a regular subject of letters between the bluestocking circle and Montagu had contacts in Paris who sent her copies of recent French publications. See Markman Ellis, 'Reading Practices in Elizabeth Montagu's Epistolary network of the 1750s' in *Bluestockings Displayed-Portraiture, Performance and Patronage 1730–1830*, ed. Elizabeth Eger (Cambridge, 2013), pp. 213–32.
14   James Boswell, *Life of Samuel Johnson* (1784), p. 213.
15   Thake, pp. 234–40.
16   *The Works of Lord Chesterfield: Including His Letters to His Son* (1838) pp. 203–4.
17   Wilmarth S. Lewis, *Horace Walpole's Library* (Cambridge, 2010), p. 8 and *Walpole Letters*, 37 vols (New Haven, 1937–83), 4, pp. 478–9, 482, 492; 5, pp. 6, 77. For Walpole's crusading ancestry, see Siberry, *Tales*, pp. 79–80.

18 Henry C. Bohn, *Catalogue of English Books on Sale in All Classes of Literature* (London, 1841), p. 1875.
19 Siberry, 'Nineteenth-Century Readers', p. 12; Royal Collection Trust. www.royalcollection.org, accessed 14 April 2023.
20 *Catalogue of the Library of the Athenaeum, Liverpool* (London, 1864); *Catalogue of the Lyceum, Liverpool* (London, 1889); https://www.theportico.org.uk, accessed 14 April 2023; *A Catalogue of the Subscription Library at Kingston upon Hull* (Hull, 1855); *Catalogue of the Library of the Writers to the Signet* (Edinburgh, 1805).
21 Henry Kett, *Elements of General Knowledge*, 6th edition (London, 1806), 2 vols, I, p. 489. Daniel Appleton, *Library Manual: Containing a Catalogue Raisonne of upwards of 12000 of the Most Important Works in Every Department of Knowledge in All Modern Languages* (New York, 1852).
22 Charles Mills, *The History of the Crusades*, 2 vols (London, 1821), I, p. vii.
23 Lord George Byron, *Letters and Journals of Lord Byron*, ed. Thomas Moore, 2 vols. (London, 1830), I, pp. 47, 83.
24 Harriet Edgeworth, *Archives and Manuscripts*. Bodleian MS Eng. Lett. 745 fol. 106–8.
25 Walter Scott, *The Siege of Malta and Bizarro*, ed. J.H. Alexander, Judy King and Graham Tulloch (Edinburgh, 2008), pp. 407, 453–62. For Scott's visit to Malta, see pp. 96–7 below.
26 Charles Knight, *Penny Cyclopaedia of the Society for the Diffusion of Useful Knowledge* (London, 1843), pp. 278–9.
27 Cecil Torr, *Rhodes in Modern Times* (Rhodes, 1881 and then Cambridge, 1887).
28 Theresa Vann, 'John Kaye, the "Dread Turk" and the siege of Rhodes', *MO* 3, 245–52; Vann and Donald J. Kagay, *Hospitaller Piety and Crusader Propaganda: Guillaume Caoursin's Description of the Ottoman Siege of Rhodes 1480* (Aldershot, 2015).
29 Vann and Kagay, p. 81.
30 *The Crusades*, ed. Alexander Murray (London, 1870).
31 *Caoursin's Account of the siege of Rhodes in 1480*, ed. Henry W. Fincham (St. John's Gate, 1926), p. 1.
32 Sir Richard Colt Hoare, *A Classical Tour through Italy and Sicily*, 2 vols (London, 1819), I, p. 275 and *Catalogue of the Colt Hoare Library at Stourhead* (1840), pp. 90 and 667; Patrick Brydone, *A tour through Sicily and Malta in a Series of Letters to William Beckford* (1773) and Donald Sultana, 'An English Antiquary in Malta', *Journal of the Faculty of Arts, Malta* 2(2), 93–105.
33 Louis de Boisgelin, *Ancient and Modern Malta and Also the History of the Knights of St John of Jerusalem*, 2 vols (London, 1804), I, pp. xv, xxiii–xli; 181–326; 2, p. i.
34 *Edinburgh Review*, 97 (1805), pp. 194–208, particularly p. 208.
35 See Scott, *Siege of Malta*, pp. 433–40.
36 James William Bryans, 'Notes on Malta and the Knights Hospitaller', *Colburn's United Service* Magazine 101 (1863), 191–205.
37 Claudius Shaw, *Sixty Years Ago; Also a Synoptical Sketch of the Order of St. John of Jerusalem from Its Foundation till the Evacuation of Malta, to Which Is Annexed a Short Sketch of the Crusades and a Concise History of the Knights Templar* (London, 1875), pp. Iv–v.
38 Charles Addison, *Damascus and Palmyra: A Journey to the East*, 2 vols (London, 1838), p. 59. See also above, pp. 19–21.
39 For example, William Robson, *Great Sieges of History* (London, 1858). The siege of Malta was also chronicled in William Prestcott's *History of the Reign of Philip II of Spain*, published in 1859–60.

40 George Percy Badger, *Description of Malta and Gozo* (1838), pp. 6, 157. For travellers to Malta, see Emanuel Chetcuti, 'The Maltese Clesse: Visitors' Impressions in Nineteenth Century Travel Narratives', *Journal of Maltese History* 5 (2018), 98–125.
41 www.royalcollection.org, accessed 14 April 2023.
42 Pâpier maché figures of knights of Maltese soldiers. LDOSJ 3013. Museum of the Order of St. John, London.
43 https://www.rmg.co.uk/objects/rmgc-object-11744, accessed 14 April 2023.
44 George F. Cruchley, *Picture of London* (London, 1842).
45 William Thackeray, *From Cornhill to Cairo* (London, 1846), p. 58.
46 Ibid, p. 58. See also Roderick Cavaliero, *The Last of the Crusaders* (London, 1960).
47 *Catalogue of the Newcastle Central Lending Library* (1908); *Catalogue of the Lyceum Liverpool* (1889).
48 *The Siege of Malta: A Fragment of the History of the Sovereign Order of St. John* (Newcastle, 1850), pp. 26–7.
49 *Saturday Review*, 24 October 1863, 557–8. The review also discussed Porter's history.
50 John Taaffe, *The History of the Holy, Military, Sovereign Order of St John of Jerusalem*, 4 vols (London, 1852).
51 *Spectator* (1852), pp. 1148 and 1853, 206.
52 See Siberry, 'John Taaffe: Poet and Historian of the Order of St. John', forthcoming *MO* 8.
53 Whitworth Porter, *A History of the Knights of Malta or the Order of St. John of Jerusalem* (London, 1858), p. 27.
54 See below, pp. 63–6.
55 *Blackwood's Magazine*, 137 (1885), 64–71.
56 See below, pp. 63–4.
57 Robert Bigsby, *Memoir of the Illustrious and Sovereign Order of St. John of Jerusalem* (Derby, 1869). See also below, p. 66.
58 Frederick Woodhouse, *The Military Religious Orders of the Middle Ages: The Hospitallers, the Templars, the Teutonic Knights and Others* (London, 1879).
59 *Encyclopaedia Britannica*, 9th edition, (1886), pp. 173–5; *Chambers Encyclopaedia* (Edinburgh, 1904), pp. 804–5.
60 *The Knights Hospitallers in England*, ed. Revd., Lambert B. Larking (Camden Society, 1857), pp. xiii, lxviii. For Larking, see Siberry, *Tales*, p. 46.
61 *The Times*, 1 May 1857, p. 5.
62 *Gentleman's Magazine*, 200 (1857), 665–70.
63 William Winthrop, 'The English, Irish and Scottish Knights of the Order of St John of Jerusalem', *Notes and Queries* 8 (1853), 189–93. For documents and related correspondence, see *Notes and Queries* 7 (1853), 407, 628–9; 8 (1853), 557–8; 9 (1854), 80–1, 99–101, 263–7, 333–4, 417–19, 442–5.
64 G.T.C. 'Notices of Such of the Family of Babington as Were of the Order of St. John of Jerusalem', *Gentleman's Magazine* 199 (1856), 564–70.
65 *English Historical Review* 11 (1896), 146–9; 13 (1898), 346–8; 15 (1900), 567–70; 17 (1902), 774–6.
66 *The Academy*, 30 April 1881, 318–19.
67 Thomas Hugo, *The History of Mynchin Buckland, Priory and Preceptory in the County of Somerset* (London, 1861); *The History of Moor Hall, a Camera of the Knights of St. John of Jerusalem* (London, 1866) and *The History of Eagle, in the County of Lincolnshire, a Commandery of the Knights Hospitallers of St. John of Jerusalem* (London, 1876).

68 W.H. Shimfield, 'On Shengay and Its Preceptory', *Proceedings of the Cambridge Antiquarian Society* 7 (1889–90), 136–47.
69 C.J. Bowden, *Hospitaller Knights of St. John of Jerusalem* (London, 1894).
70 William K.R. Bedford and Richard Holbeche, *The Order of the Hospital of St. John of Jerusalem Being a History of the English Hospitallers of St. John, Their Rise and Progress* (London, 1902).
71 Henry W. Fincham, *The Order of the Hospital of St. John of Jerusalem and Its Great Priory of England* (1915). See also https://museumstjohn.org.uk, accessed 14 April 2023.
72 Eva M. Tenison, *Chivalry and the Wounded. The Knights of St. John of Jerusalem 1014–1914* (London, 1914) and *A Short History of the Order of St. John from Its Earliest Foundation in AD 1014 to the End of the Great War of AD 1914–18* (6th edition 1922), p. 1.
73 Rose G. Kingsley, *The Order of St. John of Jerusalem Past and Present* (London, 1918), p. 18.
74 Edwin J. King, *The Knights of St. John in the British Realm* (revd. London, 1967); *The Knights Hospitallers in the Holy Land* (London, 1931); *The Seals of the Order of St. John of Jerusalem* (London, 1932); *The Knights of St. John in the British Empire* (London, 1934); *The Rules, Statutes and Customs of the Hospitallers 1099–1314* (London, 1935).
75 Augusta T. Drane, *The Knights of St. John with the Battle of Lepanto and Siege of Vienna* (London, 1858), p. iv.
76 Siberry, 'Nineteenth Century Readers', pp. 9, 16–17.
77 *The Gladstone Diaries*, ed. Henry C.G. Mathew, 17 vols (Oxford, 1994)-date entries 7/11; 14/11; 18/11; 19/11; 26/11/1842 and 8/2/1843.
78 *Edinburgh Review* 192 (1900), 45–70.
79 Ibid. The *Edinburgh Review* had also discussed Raynouard's play *Les Templiers*, See below, pp. 91–2.
80 *Eclectic Review* 12 (1842), 189–200.
81 *Athenaeum* (1842), 31–3. For Hannah Lawrance, see Siberry, *Tales*, pp. 17–18.
82 *The Court Magazine and Monthly Critic and Lady's Magazine* (1842) 22, 87–91; 23 (1843), 180.
83 Addison and Robert Macoy, *The Knights Templar and the Complete History of Masonic Knighthood from the Origins of the Orders to the Present Time* (New York, 1873).
84 Thomas Keightley, *Secret Societies of the Middle Ages* (London, 1846).
85 *Freemasons Magazine and Masonic Mirror* 463 (October 1863), 288–303, 381–4.
86 *Saturday Review*, 18 March 1865, 319–20; *Spectator*, 38 (1865), 588; *United Presbyterian Magazine* (August 1865), 368–9.
87 Andrew Favine, *The Theatre of Honour and Knighthood* (London, 1623), pp. 387–99.
88 Scott, *Ivanhoe*, ed. Graham Tulloch (Edinburgh, 1997), pp. 40, 321, 499, 503.
89 See John T. Payne, *Bibliotheca Grenvilliana* (1842); *Catalogue Library Horace Walpole*, ed. Allen T. Hazen, 3 vols (Oxford, 1969), p. 592.
90 Friedrich Munter, *Statuten buch des Ordens der Tempelherren* (Berlin, 1794); Weston S. Walford, 'On Cross-Legged Effigies Commonly Appropriated to the Templars', *Archaeological Journal* 1 (1845), 49–52.
91 Amy Grange, 'The Fall of the Knights of the Temple', *Dublin Review* 117 (1895), 329–46.
92 James A. Froude, *The Spanish Story of the Armada and Other Essays* (London, 1892), pp. 250–311.
93 Ibid., p. 310.
94 *Saturday Review*, 31 July 1886, 158–9.

95 *Good Words* 27 (1886), 378, 466, 538.

96 Revd. John Kendrick, *A Selection of Papers on Subjects of Archaeology and History Communicated to the Yorkshire Philosophical Society* (London, 1865).

97 John C. Hodgson, 'Temple Thornton Farm Accounts 1308', *Archaeologia Aeliana* 17 (1895), 40–52. See also Hodgson, "Chibburn and the Knights Hospitaller in Northumberland', *Archaeologia Aeliana* 17 (1895), 263–80.

98 S. Bentley, 'Knights Templar', *Transactions of the Bristol and Gloucestershire Archaeological Society* 18 (1893–4), 271–81.

99 James Maidment, *Papers Relative to the History, Privileges and Possessions of the Scottish Knights Templar and Their Successors, the Knights of St. John of Jerusalem* (Edinburgh, 1828–9) and *Abstract of the Charters and Other Papers Recorded in the Cartulary of Torpichen from 1581–96 with an Introductory Notice and Notes* (Edinburgh, 1830).

100 Robert Aitken, 'The Knights Templars in Scotland', *Scottish Review* (July 1898); John Edwards, 'The Templars in Scotland in the Thirteenth Century', *Scottish Historical Review* 5 (1908); Nenion Eliot, 'The Templars', *Transactions of the Hawick Archaeological Society* 19 (1877); and Alexander Walker, 'The Knights Templar in and around Aberdeen', *Aberdeen Journal*, 16 March 1887.

101 Revd. Alfred Coutts, *The Knights Templar in Scotland* (Edinburgh, 1890). See also Robert Ferguson, *The Knights Templar and Scotland* (Stroud, 2010).

102 www.theportico.org.uk, accessed 14 April 2023.

103 'The Knights Templars', *Eclectic Review* 27 (1857), 1–18. The periodical also reviewed Addison's history of the Templars and the Temple church- 12 (1842), 189–200.

104 Ferdinand Wilcke, *Geschichte des Tempelherrenordens*, 2 vols. (Leipzig, 1826–7).

105 'History of the Knights Templars', *Foreign Quarterly Review* 4 (1829), 608–41.

106 Ibid., pp. 26–9.

107 *Catalogue of the Printed Books and Manuscripts Bequeathed by Francis Douce to the Bodleian Library* (Oxford, 1840) and *Catalogue of the Valuable Library of the Late James Franck MD FRS* (1843).

108 For Mackintosh's reading, see Siberry, *Tales*, pp. 24–5.

109 *Catalogue of Hull Subscription Library* (1855).

2 Material memory

Churches and memorials

The previous chapter has illustrated how visits to Rhodes and Malta stimulated interest in the history of the Military Orders, but people did not need to travel outside Britain to be reminded of the medieval Knights of St. John and Templars. Place names throughout Britain such as Temple Sowerby, Temple Newsam, Ysbyty Ifan and Kemeys Commander recall the secular and ecclesiastical properties of the Orders, even if little or no medieval fabric has survived. There are also still a significant number of material remains, from crossed-legs effigies said to represent members of the Orders in parish churches to secular buildings such as the Cressing Temple barns. Most notably, there are four surviving round churches, in London, Cambridge, Northampton and Little Maplestead. Those who purchased properties linked with the Orders or were responsible for restoring their churches were also eager to recall the Orders' history, commissioning a variety of images of Templars and Hospitallers in stained glass and sculpture. And periodicals such as the *Gentleman's Magazine* and the journals of county antiquarian and archaeological societies enthusiastically discussed archaeological discoveries relating to the Orders.[1]

This chapter will consider first the crossed-legs effigies and the stories associated with them. It will then look at the rich history of the Temple church in London; how and why the Templars have been remembered by the knights' legal successors and the way that parallels have been drawn between past and more recent events such as the capture of Jerusalem during the First World War in December 1917. The more chequered history of the Priory building and church of St. John at Clerkenwell will also be discussed, but the use of history in connection with the nineteenth-century refurbishment of the headquarters of the revived Order will be left until the next chapter. This current chapter will finally consider the use of Templar and Hospitaller imagery in other churches and sites such as Temple Balsall, in particular in stained glass, and some more controversial excavations and discoveries.

Crossed-legs effigies

Many churches in Britain retain crossed-legs effigies which are said to represent crusaders and claims of a specific link with the Templars or, to a

DOI: 10.4324/9781003177234-3

lesser extent, Knights of St. John, first emerged in the early seventeenth century.[2] Elaborate theories were constructed to prove this link. For example, the eighteenth-century Norfolk antiquaries, Revds. Francis Blomefield and Charles Parkin, wrote a detailed account of Templar monuments in their county and claimed, when describing a chapel at South Acre, that 'to show they were not ashamed of the doctrine of the Cross, they are pourtray'd and carv'd with their legs forming a saltire cross in armour'.[3] By the 1740s this attribution was being questioned by historians of antiquities such as Richard Gough and Francis Grose, although the style was still considered to denote a crusader. And in 1820, the historian, Charles Mills, wrote that the idea that such figures represented Knights Templars 'is a notion long since exploded'.[4] It could, however, still be found in numerous county histories and correspondence between antiquaries and persists in some modern church guides. As an example of what might be termed Templar inflation, the 1831 edition of Samuel Lewis's *Topographical Dictionary of England* listed ten such effigies, but by the 1848 edition this had increased to over 60.[5]

The various attempts to revive the Military Orders and claims of unbroken continuity are discussed in Chapter 3 but, reflecting the potency of the crossed-legs 'myth', in tribute to their medieval predecessors, the members of the Templar masonic lodge at Douglas, Lanarkshire in Scotland were said in the 1860s to drink toasts with their legs crossed.[6]

The Templar association was, however, not always seen as advantageous. In 1761, Horace Walpole recorded an anecdote about the tomb of Aymer de Valence, Earl of Pembroke (d. 1324) in Westminster Abbey. There had apparently been some discussion about moving it to create space for a monument to General Wolfe, who had died in 1759 at the battle of Quebec. The Dean of Westminster agreed to the plan 'upon being told that Aymer was a Templar, a very wicked set of people', but then rescinded consent on discovering more about Aymer's history.[7]

The debate acquired a new lease of life with the restoration of the thirteenth-century effigies in the Temple church in London.[8]

Temple church, London

Over the course of its history, the Temple church in London has always attracted interest because of its architecture and monuments.[9] The poet Edmund Spenser wrote of:

> Those bricky toures
> The which on Thames brooke aged back doe ride,
> Where now the studious lawyers have their bowers
> There whilome wont the Templar knights to bide
> Till they decayed through pride.[10]

In the 1680s, Sir Christopher Wren oversaw a programme of refurbishment and the effigies were repositioned again in 1695 and on other occasions thereafter.[11] The growing interest in antiquities led to the Society of Antiquaries commissioning drawings of the eight thirteenth-century military effigies in 1718/9. They also featured in well-illustrated histories of sepulchral monuments, arms and armour, which discussed them in detail and sought to identify who they commemorated.[12]

The Temple church was mentioned as somewhere to visit in guidebooks to London and, reflecting this growing interest, an 1809 image of a group inspecting the effigies was published in Ackermann's *Microcosm of London*. The first dedicated publication, *Facts and Observations relating to the Temple church and the Monuments contained in it*, by Joseph Jekyll, a member of the Inner Temple, appeared in 1811 and in 1838, the architect Robert Billings published his *Architectural Illustrations and Account of the Temple Church* with a frontispiece depicting two Templars standing over the effigies, as if drawing back a curtain. Ghostly Templars also featured in a number of Billings's engravings of the church[13] and Charles Knight, a pioneer of illustrated publications for the general reader such as the *Penny Cyclopaedia* and *Penny Magazine*, included a short history of the Orders, illustrated by several engravings of the Temple church and a Knight Templar, in *Old England* published in 1845/6.[14] As another indicator of general interest, a painting of the Temple church, by the artist Margaret Kemp-Welch, was chosen for the library of the Doll's house commissioned by Queen Mary in the 1920s and now on display at Windsor Castle. The site also inspired Phyllis Saunders, who had grown up in the Inns of Court, to write and publish an illustrated novel featuring ghostly Templars in 1919.[15] Images of the church and the effigies were therefore widely available. They were also captured by early photography.

There are also references to the effigies in letters and novels. In 1889, the Welsh diarist and author Hester Thrale Piozzi, who claimed a crusading ancestor who had fought at Acre,[16] wrote to her niece Eva Whyte describing the 'full length figures of crusaders in brown marble [which had been] hidden away for 300 years'.[17] All visitors would have been influenced by their own interests and experience, and, as Mrs. Piozzi looked at the Temple church effigies, she may also have thought of the effigy of Sir Robert Pounderling, said to represent him as a Templar, in Tremerchion church, near her home Brynbella in Flintshire, in Wales.[18]

The effigies were also mentioned in Charles Dickens's novel *Martin Chuzzlewit*, published in 1844. His character wanders through the quiet courtyards musing upon 'darker legends of the cross-legged knights whose marble effigies were in the church'. Dickens knew the Temple well, as did his fellow author Thackeray, who was a member of the Middle Temple and resident there. He had satirised Scott's novel *Ivanhoe*, which of course featured members of the Templar Order, in his short story *Rebecca and Rowena*[19] and in *A*

Little Dinner at Timmins's, published in *Punch* in 1848, the aspiring poetess Mrs. Timmins has notepaper stamped with:

> the hand and battleaxe, the crest of the Timminses (and borne at Ascalon by Roaldus de Timmins, a crusader who is now buried in the Temple church, next to Sergeant Snooks).[20]

Thackeray was obviously poking fun at the contemporary desire to claim a noble crusading ancestor, but he was also interested in the genuine history of the Military Orders and visited Rhodes and Malta, as well as the Holy Land, Egypt and Syria in 1844/5.[21] The records of the London Library show that he borrowed books on crusade history and he knew the lawyer and historian Charles Addison.[22] Antiquarians were keen to source and display items relating to the Orders and in his novel *The Antiquary*, Walter Scott, a keen collector of medieval artefacts himself, made Jonathan Oldbuck exclaim:

> Lord deliver me from this Gothic generation…a monument of a knight templar on each side of a Grecian porch and a Madonna on the top.[23]

The interest in the effigies could result in some curious requests. In his five volume work *Sepulchral Effigies*, published between 1788 and 1796, Richard Gough recounted 'on good authority' that:

> Application was made by a Hertfordshire baronet for some of these cross legged knights to grace his new erected parochial church; but the Society of Benchers discovered their good sense, as well as regard to antiquity, by refusing their compliance.[24]

This story was also recounted in the *Gentleman's Magazine*, which reflected on the change in attitude towards such monuments:

> At the present moment, the absurdity of the application (now apparent to all, but seemingly then refused without any expression of surprise), induces involuntarily a smile; and this anecdote is therefore interesting, as affording one example, among many, of the vast change in public opinion relative to the works of our forefathers, which has taken place so happily and so universally, within a few years.[25]

Knights and lawyers

Rosemary Sweet has described the evolution of attitudes towards the church:

> In the early eighteenth century it was primarily a memorial to the lawyers of the Inns of Court and a reminder of the extent to which the Great Fire had ravaged London. The knights' tombs were of interest chiefly for their

connection with the nobility of thirteenth century England. As a structure, it was a minor curiosity; its physical appearance obscured by modern accretions; and, without the vocabulary to describe what was there, it was not possible for written descriptions to realize its form with any greater clarity. By the early nineteenth century it was renowned both for the knights' tombs and as an illustration of the historical evolution of Gothic architecture.[26]

In parallel, there was growing interest in the history of the Templars because of their role during the crusades and later fate. The historiography of the Military Orders has been discussed in Chapter 1, but many of the early antiquaries were also lawyers[27] and several histories of the Order and church were written by members of the legal profession who lived and worked in the Inns of Court in London.

For example, the historiography of the Temple church included works by William Burge Q.C, a barrister as well as a Fellow of the Society of Antiquaries (FSA), who had strong views on the nature of worship and layout of the church and published *The Temple Church: an Account of its Restoration and Repairs* in 1843. And in 1845, another member of the Middle Temple was inspired to put pen to paper by claims that the Temple church effigies represented Templars. He sought to disprove this theory and did so in a way which suggested detailed research on the subject.[28] Fifty years later, Henry Baylis Q.C., a Bencher of the Inner Temple and Council Member of the Royal Archaeological Institute, published a guide to the church.[29] The subject also attracted the interest of another member of the Inner Temple, Hugh Bellot, who chronicled its literary, legal and historic associations and his detailed bibliography shows that discussions about the Temple church fabric and restorations could be found in various legal magazines.[30]

John Yonge Anderson Morshead, another Middle Temple lawyer, antiquary and cousin of the writer Charlotte Yonge, turned his legal skills to a survey of the evidence adduced in the Templars' trial and the way in which it had been interpreted by historians such as Jules Michelet and Joseph von Hammer Purgstall. His analysis, published under the name J. Shallow (presumably a Shakesperian pun), indicated that he had read a range of publications in German and French, as well as English, and argued for the availability of more original sources. The legal publishers Stevens and son advertised it as seeking to 'clear up some of the mystery' and 'refute some of the current theories'.[31] Morshead's efforts, however, were dismissed by the *Saturday Review:*

> Mr Shallow has read a good deal about the abolition of the Order of the knight Templar and has given us the results of his reading in such an incoherent fashion that it would be less troublesome, as well as infinitely

more profitable, to read the authors he quotes than to seek to understand his comments upon them.[32]

An architectural historian has suggested that the:

> Benchers' interest was secular, historical and corporate or professional… Temple church with its recumbent knights was a tangible expression of the Benchers' corporate identity and Royal Privilege. It was also a symbol of the continuity of the professional history and its independence.[33]

Some other examples of explicit linkages between the medieval past and legal present will be discussed later, but it inspired some more humorous comparisons. In 1803, the artist James Sayers, who had trained as a lawyer, but decided to focus on political caricature, produced an etching entitled *The Master of the Inn confers the Order of Knighthood of Don Quixote*, which showed the Lord Chief Justice, Sir James Mansfield, knighting James St. Clair Erskine, who fought in the French Revolutionary Wars, as an officer in the Inns of Court Volunteers. The scene takes place in the cloister of the Temple church and in the background, three recumbent Templars look on in apparent horror. Words below urge the valiant Templars of old 'to sleep in peace…nor cast a look beyond the grave, to mark our Inn's dishonour' (Figure 2.1).[34]

Visiting writers and artists from America and Europe also left their impressions of the church. For example, Alexander Lesser, from Poland, made several drawings of the knights which are now in the collection of the Warsaw Museum[35] and in 1849, the American novelist Herman Melville, now better known as the author of the novel *Moby Dick*, 'saw the ten crusaders-those who had been to the Holy Land, with their legs crossed'. Some years later, he published a story in *Harper's New Monthly Magazine* entitled *The Paradise of Bachelors* in which he encouraged fellow New Yorkers to see 'the wondrous tombs' while musing on the Templars' successors:

> The iron heel is changed to a boot of patent leather; the long two-handed sword to a one-handed quill; the monk-giver of gratuitous ghostly counsel now counsels for a fee…the vowed opener and clearer of all highways leading to the Holy Sepulchre, now has it in particular charge to check, clog… and embarrass all the courts and avenues of law; the Knight-combatant of the Saracen, breasting spear-point at Acre, now fights law-points in Westminster Hall…the Templar is today a Lawyer.[36]

Melville's story had a serious purpose and was published in tandem and to contrast with *Tartarus of Maids*, which described the lives of female workers in a New England paper factory.

*Figure 2.1 The Master of the Inn confers the Order of Knighthood on Don Quixotte.
Print by James Sayers. Royal Collection Trust/© His Majesty King Charles
III 2023.*

Restoration

The controversial programme of restoration of the church in the 1840s fuelled
interest in the Templars.[37] Not all approved of the work, but Robert Mudie,
editor of *Architect, Engineer and Surveyor*, wrote:

Many (buildings) have been either partially or entirely reconstructed with greater or less effect, but none so completely or with so much taste as the Temple church...though the critic may find something to blame, he must be of a more morbid temperament than is common to even that class if he does not admit that there is much more to approve.[38]

The *Gentleman's Magazine* commented:

Whoever remembers the Temple church in all its former glories of white-washed ceilings and pillars and naked ground glass windows, who was annoyed with the glare of light...will at once see how justly the ancient edifices were designed to receive its stained glass windows.[39]

Artefacts found during the work were also the subject of discussion among archaeologists writing in the *Gentleman's Magazine*.[40]

The Times praised the restoration and recalled the church's original occupants:

If the mind could not altogether exclude the recollections of those mis-guided warriors, whose name and whose memory yet linger in the spot which centuries ago their stern enthusiasm hallowed...so amid the peaceful fraternities that have succeeded them...there survives among the modern Templars all the high and honourable feeling (without the accompanying delusions) which for the most part characterized the Templars of old.[41]

The service to celebrate the reopening of the church in November 1842 was attended by members of the British royal family and the *Illustrated London News* declared:

As public journalists, it has seldom been our pleasing duty to record an event of greater interest to all lovers of antiquity than that afforded by the magnificent repair and restoration of the Temple church.[42]

The resulting Victorian church fabric and decoration were completely de-stroyed in the bombing on the night of 10 May 1941 and some did not lament their loss. The Treasurer of the Inner Temple, Sir Frank Mackinnon, wrote:

Seeing how dreadfully the Church had been despoiled by its pretended friends a century before, I do not grieve so very acutely for the havoc now wrought by its avowed enemies...If the church is now once again truly re-stored, it can hardly fail to be far more beautiful than the Victorian vandals made it for us. To have got rid of their awful stained glass windows...will be almost a blessing in disguise.[43]

The present East window, a gift from the Glaziers' Company and designed by Carl Edwards, however, still evokes the church's knightly history with images of the Templars and key figures in their history.

Fashions and opinions may change, but the 1840s restoration is worth revisiting because it was carried out by some of the major artists and designers of the day and reflects how they then wished to depict and commemorate the Templars.

One of the artists involved in the church restoration was Thomas Willement, a leading stained glass designer. The subjects of his East windows were:

> Geoffrey, son of Stephen and Amaric de St. Maur, Grand Preceptors of the Order in England; the arms of Henry I and Baldwin, King of Jerusalem; the red cross of the Templars; two knights riding on the same horse as represented on the first seal of the Knights Templar; Alanus Marcel and Robert de Monfort, Grand Preceptors of England.

Willement was also responsible for the mural decoration and on the arch between the round and the nave, he painted six enthroned figures of the English monarchs connected with the history of the Templars, including:

> Henry I in whose reign the order was first recognised;
> Henry II with a representation of the Temple church as it was built in his reign;
> Coeur de Lion "the only monarch of England who was personally engaged in the crusades."

Drawings of these representations of the Templars have survived in a book published in 1845, with an account of the restoration, by the architect Sydney Smirke.[44]

The military effigies in the church were also restored in the 1840s, with similar controversy, by Edward Richardson. He made casts that were displayed outside the Romanesque and Byzantine Court in an exhibition at Crystal Palace, London, which opened in 1854. The casts survived the fire of 1936 and can now be seen in the cast court of the Victoria and Albert Museum and the Temple church. There was also at least one other set of casts commissioned by the Temple church architect Lewis Cottingham, which have not survived. As already noted, illustrations and photographs of the effigies were published in a wide range of publications, from books to magazines and, correctly or incorrectly described as Templars, they would have played an important part in shaping the public image of members of the Order.[45]

Inner Temple Hall

The opening of the new Inner Temple Hall by Queen Victoria's daughter, Princess Louise, in May 1870, inspired a poem published in the satirical magazine *Punch*:

> From mail to gown, from prayers to pleas; from arms to wordy war,
> Strangely time's whirly gig hath spun alongside Temple Bar
> Since "Christ's poor soldiers" the white robe with the red cross did don…
> Still stands the Temple as before…but mail is turned to miniver.[46]

The Temple complex included other depictions of the knights. In 1875, the sculptor Henry Armstead, whose work can also be seen on, for example, the Albert Memorial in Kensington, designed four life size bronze statues of two Templars and two Hospitallers as part of the decoration of the refurbished Inner Temple Hall. The correspondence between Armstead and the Treasurer of the Inner Temple as the commission evolved has survived in the Inner Temple archives and at one stage the design included a frieze drawing the link between the medieval and modern uses of the site:

> The ancient and modern uses of the Foundation might be shown by having on the one hand a procession of Knights Templar protecting pilgrims on their way to the Holy Land and on the other Moses, or some other great lawgiver expounding the law.

The frieze was not commissioned, but the final design of the Hall drew a parallel between past and present, with the great West window showing Queen Victoria with the four virtues representing Law and Government and other windows with scenes from English history.[47]

The knights were initially intended to be displayed on brackets high up on the walls, but in 1886, the Treasurer of the Temple instructed that they should be placed where they could be better seen and appreciated.

Armstead's statues were destroyed in the May 1941 bombing, but there is a dramatic, albeit rather staged, picture of them amidst the rubble (Figure 2.2).

The effigies have continued to inspire artists and a window engraved by Laurence Whistler, in 1962, in the church at Checkendon in Oxfordshire, to commemorate the artist Eric Kennington, best known perhaps for his effigy of T.E. Lawrence in Wareham, Dorset, depicts two knights modelled on the Temple effigies. Kennington and Lawrence had become close friends, sharing a passion for medieval architecture and towards the end of Lawrence's life they were collecting photographs and information for a book on the subject.[48]

Figure 2.2 The Inner Temple Hall after the May 1941 bomb. Courtesy of the Benchers of the Honourable Society of the Inner Temple.

Linking past and present: commemorative services

As has already been noted, the legal residents of the Temple took an interest in their knightly predecessors and on 1 and 8 March 1885, services were held in the Temple church commemorating the 700th anniversary of its consecration by Patriarch Heraclius of Jerusalem. The service on 1 March was attended by the Prince and Princess of Wales and various other dignitaries, with a sermon preached by the Archbishop of Canterbury, Edmund Benson. A week later, the Master of the Temple, Charles Vaughan, preached to a congregation of members of the Inner and Middle Temples.

Commemorating the 1185 foundation of the Temple church, as well as recalling the recent events in the Sudan, the Archbishop declared:

> Is not the chivalry of the West as ready as ever to shatter itself today against the valour of the desert …England has marked with awe the spirit of the man who went single handed to the fight…our soldier martyr…Khartoum is one more tragic scene in the tale of Tiberias and Acre.

And he went on to make a link between the past and present occupants of the Temple:

> Their empty halls were immediately repeopled with a new chivalry of justice, peace, order, reason- in one word, of Law.

He added that St. Louis's Sainte Chapelle in Paris was similarly 'assigned to the life and work of the lawyers of France'.

All the addresses drew links between contemporary events and the history of the Templars and crusades and the theme of Christian heroism and sacrifice had a particular resonance with the death of General Gordon at Khartoum.[49] Gordon had been killed on 26 January 1885, but news took some time to reach Britain. He was soon remembered and praised as a Christian hero and the Temple service took place against this background and shortly before a national day of mourning, on 13 March, followed by a memorial service at St. Paul's cathedral.[50]

The address by Revd Alfred Ainger, Reader at the Temple church, was entitled *The Knights of the Red Cross* and he reminded the congregation of the history of the Templars and the church in which they all worshipped:

> This church, in which such myriads of men have met for worship, through the ages of Plantagenet and Tudor, Stuart and Hanoverian, is indissolubly connected in name as well as history with the famous Order which erected it. Although dedicated to the Blessed Virgin, the name of its Patron Saint has never deposed from the memory and imagination of Englishmen the name of that far off Temple in Palestine, within whose precincts the small and devoted band of warriors found shelter.

Ainger spoke of the ways in which the ideal of the Christian knight had changed over the intervening seven centuries and once again praised the Christian heroism and service of Gordon:

> A nobler image of the Christian soldier than the most valiant, the most religious of the Knights of the Temple ever supplied, is shown in the person of our ideal knight, who by his life and death, for all Christendom,

has elevated men's conceptions of the possibilities of the union of soldier and saint.

He again drew parallels between the knights and their legal successors:

> The Temple of today is rich in inheritance and survival from the Temple of Henry II. We worship in their church; the Hall of the Inner Temple stands on the site of the refectory of the knights; the arms of the Treasurers ranged along its walls are lineal successors of the shields of the knights; the brothers of the legal order still take their chief meal in common.[51]

The Master of the Temple, Dr. Charles Vaughan, looked back to the days of the Templars, but also imagined a future service in the church, in which those present would recollect the day 'when they heard an English archbishop commemorate the historical act of a Palestinian patriarch' in the presence of the heir to the throne. Vaughan proposed three maxims-interrogate the past; occupy the present and trust the future. He then drew parallels between the medieval and modern Templars:

> Brethren Templars of the present, is it not that the very thing which makes your occupancy of these courts and halls, of this ancient church itself, so suitable...the protection of weakness against brute force, the securing of the imperilled rights from aggression and from the oppression of the wrong.

Vaughan praised their charitable work in East London and once again reminded the congregation of Gordon:

> This was the work of our last hero...when he gave himself to the seeking and saving of the waifs and strays of London, as he would fain have given himself afterwards to the protection of the poor sheep (as he called them) of the Soudan.

Vaughan concluded by stating that England would weather the storms of the present and future as she had weathered the storms of the past.[52]

Both services were reported in the national and regional newspapers and periodicals of the day[53] and the *Saturday Review* commended the parallels drawn between 'the great Christian hero who has just fallen at Khartoum' and 'the Templars who fell in battle with the infidel at Acre and Tiberias'.[54] The 1185 consecration was also depicted in a rather romanticised painting of 1912 by the artist Maud Tindal Atkinson, the daughter and sister of lawyers.[55]

First World War

Following the capture of Jerusalem by General Allenby, the *Times* announced a special service in the church in view of its 'historical associations' and 'the religious significance of the British occupation'.[56] Held on 16 December 1917, the sermon was given by the Master of the Temple, Revd. E.W. Barnes, who later became Bishop of Birmingham. He noted:

> We cannot meditate on the capture of Jerusalem without thinking of that great Order, splendid in its inception, dramatic in its fall, to which we owe this noble building.

He then proceeded to remind the congregation of the history of the foundation of the Order of the Temple, drawing on William of Tyre, Gibbon and more recently Addison's history and wreaths of laurel were placed upon the knights' effigies. Barnes drew parallels with the Templar's Red Cross and the 'accepted sign of our own efforts to alleviate the suffering of the battlefield'. Recalling the circumstances which had led to the fall of the Templars, the Master expressed the hope that 'our nation keep more truly than they the ideal of their founders' and he concluded by celebrating the news of Jerusalem's capture:

> Once again the object of the crusaders is accomplished, and the Holy Sepulchre is under Christian control. None surely is so poor in imagination as to fail to be thrilled by the thought; none who come to worship in the Temple church, who on their way pass the recumbent figures of the crusading knights who have lain here for some 700 years-across their breasts the laurel fitly lies today-none can forget the past or fail to pray that we may be worthy of the trust committed to our charge.[57]

The sermon was published the following year at the request of the Middle and Inner Temples.

In February 1918, the Treasurer of the Inner Temple, Charles Darling, later a High Court judge and Lord Darling, published a poem 'To the Soldiers of the Temple' in the *Saturday Review*, which similarly drew parallels between the service of the medieval Templars and their modern successors:

> Ye left our knightly fare and Common Hall
> As erst those Templars who, with hearts elate,
> Did 'neath the cross the Crescent's pride abate,
> For Christ's high law content in fight to fall.
>
> Though some are fallen Jordan or Aisne along
> Your laurels deck the tombs of those old knights
> Who Beauseant planted where ye kneel today.
> Justice arisen, and ordered freedom strong,
> The Templars' service, as their death, requites,
> Who left the happier took the holier way.[58]

This poem was later included in Darling's book listing Templars who had served in the Great War.[59]

After the disastrous bombing in May 1941, the Temple church seems to have been used as a vehicle to underline the continuity of struggle and boost morale. A montage, now said to be in the Guildhall collection in London, shows warriors in the roofless round, from the Templars of old through to the service men and women of the 1940s. Its purpose and message were that the war was a new crusade and it encouraged those who had inherited the church to match the resilience and Christian values of those who built it.[60]

Priory of St. John at Clerkenwell

St. John's Gate, now familiar as the headquarters of the Order of St. John, has had a mixed and colourful history. After the dissolution of the Order in 1540 it was used for storage of royal possessions and then as the office of the Master of the Revels, who presided over the production of plays, including the works of William Shakespeare. By the early eighteenth century, it was a coffee house owned by the father of the artist William Hogarth and the place where the popular *Gentleman's Magazine*, often quoted in this book as a source of contemporary antiquarian debate and discovery, was first launched and published. There were echoes of the crusading past with part of the building becoming The Old Jerusalem tavern, decorated with suits of armour and selling its 'chivalerie' gin.[61]

A society known as the Knights of St. John of Jerusalem was founded in 1826 by a W.M. Humphris. It met at St. John's Gate every Monday evening for conversation, supper and singing, drawing on the medieval Order's history for its ceremonies and dress code and by 1840 was said to have had a membership of over 1,000. A brief history of the knights and the buildings at Clerkenwell by a W. Till, who had a business selling medals and coins, was published in London in 1834. It celebrated the 'social, philanthropic and brotherly Knights' who were 'considered to take precedence of almost every other in London [and] intended as a copy of the ancient Order of knighthood'.[62] The book's frontispiece by the caricaturist Robert Cruikshank depicted 'an animated representation of the modern Society of the Knights of St. John, as they appear at their convivial meeting on the Monday evening'. The Grand Master sits centre stage, with armoured figures of earlier Grand Priors of England, Sir William Weston and Sir Thomas Docwra, on the walls, and he is surrounded by members in evening dress (Figure 2.3).

In 1873, however, the Gate's fortunes changed when its freehold was acquired by one of the key figures in the revival of the modern Order, Sir Edmund Lechmere and its refurbishment, with a close eye to history, has been described by Nigel Hankin and is discussed in the following chapter.[63]

The fate of St. John's church involved its demolition in the reign of Edward VI; rebuilding in the eighteenth century, but then acquisition by Lechmere and restoration as the Order's church, reopening in 1901. Like the Temple church,

Figure 2.3 'An animated representation of the modern Society of the Knights of St. John, as they appear at their convivial meeting on the Monday evening'. Frontispiece by Robert Cruikshank to W. Till's *A Concise History of the Ancient and Illustrious Order of the Knights Hospitallers of St. John of Jerusalem, Rhodes and Malta*, (London, 1834). Courtesy of Chetham's Library, Manchester.

it suffered badly in the bombing of central London in May 1941, before further restoration in its present form.

Cambridge, Northampton and Little Maplestead

Apart from the Temple church, there are 15 confirmed round church sites in England in towns, cities and rural villages.[64] Three still survive in Cambridge, Northampton and Little Maplestead. In 1807, the antiquary John Britton published an early essay on their architecture in his *Antiquities of Britain*, although he does not seem to have had a high opinion of either the Templars or the crusades, citing Gibbon as a recommended source of information:

> For the most luminous and unprejudiced history of the "quixotic crusaders" and their devastating expeditions, misnomered "holy wars", see Gibbon's Decline and Fall of the Roman Empire.[65]

All underwent substantial restoration in the nineteenth century, with varying degrees of controversy and different approaches to their history.[66]

The restoration of the church of the Holy Sepulchre in Cambridge by the Camden Society did not include any attempts to represent members of the

Military Orders, but at the Church of the Holy Sepulchre in Northampton, which became a garrison church for the local army regiment, several war memorial windows evoke the past history of the crusades more generally.

The history of the Hospitaller church at Little Maplestead inspired the young architect William Wallen, who published an illustrated history of the church that included a lengthy prefatory history of the crusades.[67] Wallen's motivation was 'to excite and increase interest in favour of the preservation of Little Maplestead church' and his lengthy subscriber list included over 100 architects ranging from Augustus Pugin to John Nash and Sir John Soane.[68] Wallen concluded:

> If, by the present work, the attention of the public be directed to the dilapidated condition of the church at Little Maplestead, the object we have in view will be attained. There are not many such remains of antiquity, and for that reason we have here given some draughts of it; to which we were the more inclined, because it is possible it may ere long be levelled, and not only the figure of it forgot, but the very place also where it stood.[69]

A poem was also published in 1850 to raise funds for the restoration. The unnamed poetess, from the neighbouring rectory of Wickham St. Paul, who clearly knew the sixteenth-century Italian poet Tasso's epic poem about the First Crusade, declared:

> Memorial of a nation's
> We ask a nation's aid
> Fain would we, in such a holy cause,
> Invoke a fresh crusade.[70]

Wallen's footnotes reveal extensive research and he stated that he planned to complete similar histories of the churches in London, Cambridge and Northampton, but ill health led to his retirement in 1853.

A review in the *Athenaeum* questioned whether Wallen had added much to the existing state of knowledge and suggested that he divert his energies elsewhere:

> With the enthusiasm of an intellectual follower of his art [he]enlists as subservient to his subject, the history of the splendid and warlike Order of the Knights Hospitaller. The history, indeed, of the church itself, and the description of its architectural peculiarities, does not occupy more than a fifth of the volume; in fact, we have little more than what Mr. Britton has already given us in his Architectural Antiquities.
>
> Mr. Wallen…promises to complete the history and antiquities of the remaining round churches… but we would advise one so zealous and able in the cause not to occupy his time on subjects already well illustrated.[71]

Wallen's fears of destruction were not realized, but he may not have agreed with the extensive restoration which took place from 1851–7. Little Maplestead, however, remains very much part of the history of the Order of St. John, with an annual service taking place there every year.

Other churches: stained glass

Images of knights in stained glass in churches and secular buildings linked with the Orders were another way of remembering them and there are examples of this throughout Britain, commissioned by individual churches and landowners, who were keen to celebrate the history of their estates using leading designers and glass manufacturers of the day. As already discussed, both images and text have shaped the memory of the Military Orders and the designers tasked with these commissions would have drawn on sources such as the history of costume in England published by Frederick Fairholt in 1846, Samuel Meyrick's 1824 history of armour and the drawings of the knights by the English army officer, artist and naturalist Charles Hamilton Smith. These books would probably have been on the shelves of the firms involved, although records have sadly not survived to tell the story from initial concept to the commission, design, manufacture and installation of the various windows. Individual engravings of the knights from these works were also widely reproduced.[72]

Templars: Cornwall, Warwickshire, Yorkshire, Pembrokeshire and Gloucestershire

The stained glass designed by Thomas Willement for the Temple church has already been mentioned, but several other churches with Templar associations were restored in the nineteenth century and their benefactors chose to include images of these knightly predecessors. Thus, the small church of Temple, near Bodmin in Cornwall, has a small window in the North Tower depicting a Templar on horseback, which was the gift of a local firm.[73] A service of consecration for the restored church took place in May 1883, with a sermon by the Bishop of Truro, Edmund Benson, who as Archbishop of Canterbury later presided over the Temple church service in 1885.

At St. Mary's, Temple Balsall, which was restored by Sir George Gilbert Scott in the 1840s, the striking East window, dating from 1907, was designed by James Powell, a well-established London-based firm. It depicts both a Templar and Hospitaller, under the badges of their Orders and beneath the figures there are the heraldic arms of the last two Grand Priors of the Order of St. John in England, Thomas Dowcra and William Weston. The corbels supporting the chapel roof, designed by the London firm Philip Wynne and Lumsden, also depict knights and are said to have been based on the effigies in the Temple church, further underlining their influence in the developing image of the Templar.[74]

At Temple Grafton, the new owner of the estate, James William Carlile, who had made his fortune as a Yorkshire based thread manufacturer, had a strong interest in history and archaeology. He funded the rebuilding of the church in 1875 and employed the architect and stained glass designer Frederick Preedy. The West window again celebrates the history of both Orders, with a Templar and Hospitaller and smaller images of the knights tending the sick and protecting pilgrims. The chancel tiles also depict a Templar knight. Carlile therefore made sure that later worshippers and visitors to the church understood the history of the site and it is probably no coincidence that his coat of arms included a cross and crescent, symbols often used to reflect a link with the crusades.[75]

Thomas Willement was also responsible for another window dated 1852 depicting a Templar and Hospitaller in the chapel of St. Andrew attached to Ribston Hall, a former Templar property, in Yorkshire. The Hall had been purchased in 1836 by Joseph Dent, another keen antiquarian, so it is again not surprising that he decided to reflect the history of his new residence. He also included some Templar shields.[76]

Elsewhere the local link and choice had a different origin, At St. James's church, Manorbier in Pembrokeshire, the birthplace of Gerald of Wales, whose *Itinerarium Cambriae* was an account of the preaching tour of Archbishop Baldwin of Canterbury before the Third Crusade, two local men returning safely from service in the Red Cross in France and Italy chose Hugh Paganis (Hugh of Payns) together with Alfred the Great for a window produced by the firm of James Powell and designed by Arthur Van Daele.[77]

The reason for the choice of the figure of a Templar, paired with St. Michael, in a window at the church of St. Mary the Virgin, St. Briavels, Gloucestershire, by the designer Arthur Louis Moore dated 1922, is less clear. It commemorates a local resident, Colonel Gervas Selwyn Eyre, who served in the army in India and Burma and died aged 69 in 1920. It may simply be a further example of how widespread interest in the Order and its military history had become.[78]

Knights of St. John: Cardiff, Wiltshire, Herefordshire and Sussex

Mention as already been made of windows depicting both Templars and Hospitallers, but the Order of St. John was also celebrated specifically in stained glass. In Cardiff, the church of St. John has a twentieth-century chapel dedicated to the Order of St. John and the Priory of Wales, which had been established in 1918 with the Prince of Wales as its Prior. A four light window by James Powell depicts four figures from the history of the Order, including Grand Masters Philip de Villiers and Jean de La Valette.[79] The noble service of the knights was also drawn upon to commemorate those who had died in the First World War, with, for example, a Hospitaller knight included in a memorial window in the church of St. James, Devizes, Wiltshire.[80]

Dinmore and Hereford

At Dinmore in Herefordshire, a former Commandery of the Knights Hospitaller, its history was enthusiastically celebrated in stained glass and statues in the Music Room and Cloisters built by the owner in the 1930s, Richard Hollins Murray, himself a proud member of the Order. The bronze figures of a Hospitaller and Templar are said to resemble those in the Inner Temple destroyed in 1941. The medieval chapel had been restored by a previous owner, Revd. Harris Fleming St. John, in 1886.[81] The chapel of the medieval St. John Hospital in Hereford also includes a window celebrating the Order, which came from the chapel of Harewood House. Harewood's then owner, Chandos Hungerford Hoskyns, had commissioned the architect William Rushworth to rebuild the estate chapel in 1862, in a style which reflected its previous ownership by the Templars then Hospitallers. Like many other great houses, Harewood was demolished in the 1950s.[82]

Archaeological discoveries and controversies

Church restorations provided another opportunity to celebrate the history of the Orders and produced some interesting and sometimes controversial archaeological discoveries.

The Stock Gaylard Templar

In 1884, the children of Mr. and Mrs. Harry Yeatman decided to restore the church of St. Barnabas church, Stock Gaylard, Dorset, in their parents' memory. Beneath a stone effigy of a cross-legged knight, known to the family as the Knight Templar effigy, they found a dismembered skeleton and some scraps of red leather. Contemporary notes by Lewys Legge Yeatman speculated that the Templar's bones had been brought back from Palestine in a leather case. They also described a ceremony, attended by the family, in which the bones were placed in a new wooden coffin bearing a red Templar cross in a burial service on Sunday 31 August 1884. The local builder's bill for the 'new box for the Knight Templar's bones' and vault came to ten shillings.[83]

The Templar is said to be Sir Ingelramus de Waleys, Lord of the Manor, who it was claimed had died fighting in Jerusalem in 1274, but the basis for this identification is questionable and has been challenged by some historians.

In his history of Dorset, published in 1774, John Hutchins described the monument in the church as follows:

> In an indented gothic arch in the North wall of the body is the stone effigy of a man recumbent, completely armed, with a triangular shield girded over his shoulder, a helmet without a visor, and a long flat sword on which he rests his right hand. His legs are crossed, and his feet are supported by a lion couchant. From his habit he appears to have been a knight templar or a crusader. From his figure being placed in the wall of the church, it is most probably the monument of the founder whose body it was antiently the custom to bury on the foundation, Tradition says it was the monument of Sir Ingelramus de Walys Kt died 32E, but it is more probably of a much older date.[84]

Hutchins initially also identified the effigy at Milton Abbey as a crusader or Knight Templar because of the crossed-legs, but he later deleted the Templar attribution.[85]

Rothley

The Templars had acquired their preceptory at Rothley Temple in Leicestershire through John de Harcourt, who had died on the Fifth Crusade at Damietta.[86] It then became the property of the Hospitallers and after that the Babington family, whose numbers included several Knights of St. John.[87] The fabric of the Templar chapel survived through the centuries, but the fate of a crossed-legs effigy, said to represent a Templar, illustrates changing historical fashion. Mentioned and illustrated by John Nicholls in his 1782 *History and Antiquities of Leicestershire*, it had already been removed from the church, but Nicholls suggested that:

> It would be highly creditable to the cultivated talents of the present owner if so remarkable a relique of the Templars were again restored to its former situation. A very small sum would replace it in a manner that would reflect honour on the lord of the soke.[88]

By the early twentieth century, parts of the effigy were serving as moss covered stones in a rockery, but it is now protected and displayed in the chapel of the Rothley Court Hotel, whose owner in the late 1950s was himself a member of the modern Templar Order. There are also images of a Hospitaller and Templar in stained glass on the stairwell of the hotel, probably dating from the restoration of the house and chapel by the Manchester architect John Ely for its then owner, the German born cotton merchant Frederick Marttens, and modern tapestries in the chapel depicting Templars.[89]

Physical remains were not the only way in which the Templar past was recalled. In 1815, Rothley's Templar history inspired the Revd. Thomas Gisborne to write a poem about the crusades, entitled *Rothley Temple*, which he dedicated to his brother-in-law, Thomas Babington MP, the owner of Rothley and a fellow antislavery campaigner. Gisborne wrote of Babington 'in whose life are portrayed all the qualities of his supposed predecessor Sir Godfrey de Babington not essential to the military character of a Knight Templar' and the poem celebrates the crusading feats of the said Sir Godfrey as a member of the Lord Edward's crusade.[90] It is questionable whether such a crusader existed, but it gave the Revd. Gisborne a vehicle to pay tribute to his friend and the theme of the poem- a returned orphaned crusader fighting for the return of his property – appealed to the nineteenth-century poet and reader.

Danbury

The knightly effigies and 'pickled corpse' uncovered in St. John's church in Danbury, Essex in 1779, prompted some colourful correspondence in the *Gentleman's Magazine*. The claim was made, again seemingly on the basis that the effigy had crossed-legs, that this was another Templar burial. The report by a T. White described the opening of the coffin in some detail:

> Whether the legs were crossed or not, must for ever remain a doubt, though I am strongly of the opinion that they were, for one of the gentlemen pushing a walking stick rather briskly from the knees to the ankles, the left foot separated from the leg somewhere about the ankle.

After these basic and rather brutal tests had been made, the church doors were apparently opened to allow the parishioners to satisfy their curiosity before the coffin was resealed.[91] The effigies would have been familiar to many more through engravings in publications such as Richard Gough's *Sepulchral Effigies* and Joseph Strutt's *Costumes of England*.

Once again, the Templar attribution is questionable. In his history of Essex, published in 1768, Philip Morant, unpicked the crusading claim:

> In the north wall of the north aisle of the church are two arches, in each of which is a man in armour, cut in wood, lying upon his back, and cross legged, which is a sign that they were engaged in the crusades. According to tradition, they are two of the Darcies. But it is more likely that they belong to the St. Clares, who held land here from K. Stephen to Edward the second's time, when the holy war was in vogue and probably founded this north aisle. Whereas the first of the Darcys who had Danbury dyed in 1428, which was 137 years after the end of the Holy war.[92]

It is unclear whether the enthusiastic Mr. White knew of Morant's analysis and the latter's history of the St. Clere family makes no reference to a crusader or Templar. But it remained a good story.

Temple Bruer

The excavations at Temple Bruer proved more controversial. In 1841, the Revd. Dr. George Oliver of nearby Scopwick undertook a survey of the Templar site at Temple Bruer in Lincolnshire. He believed that he had found underground chambers and the presence of some bones and burnt material led him to conclude that this had been the scene of Templar crimes:

> The ruins exhibit woeful symptoms of crime and unfair dealing. We can scarcely forbear entertaining the opinion that these are the crumbling remains of unhappy persons, who had been confined in the dungeons of the preceptory; for the Templars and their successors were always in feud with their neighbours and would not be very likely to remit what they might conceive to be the merited punishment of delinquency.

The series of unfounded assumptions, later shared in a talk to the Lincolnshire Topographical Society, says something about Oliver's view of the Templars. A later excavation, however, by W.H. St. John Hope and published in *Archaeologia* in 1905, dismissed these claims and suggested that the supposed dungeon was more prosaically the foundations of the presbytery.[93]

Rosslyn chapel

Any discussion of the material memory of the Orders must also make some reference to Rosslyn chapel in Scotland. Founded as a collegiate church by William Sinclair in the mid-fifteenth century, there is no substantiated Templar link. Nevertheless, Rosslyn has accrued many stories and claims connected with the Templars, perpetuated in modern guidebooks, novels and films. It was much visited by romantic poets and artists and the French artist and photographer Louis Daguerre's *Interior of Roslin chapel* depicted two figures in white with the red Templar cross.[94]

Conclusion

The material legacy of the Templars and Hospitallers is both rich and varied, from sculpted crossed-legs effigies to churches, which were once the property of the Orders and whose nineteenth-century restorations provided an opportunity to include romanticised images of the knights, particularly in stained glass. The prime example is obviously the Temple church in London, visited by many and known to others through guidebooks and histories of the Templar Order. Material memories of the Military Orders could and can, however, be seen throughout Britain. Specific links were also made between past and present with celebrations of key anniversaries. Thus, the Temple church was the venue for celebratory services in 1885, 700 years after the visit of the Patriarch Heraclius and 1917/8 following the recapture of Jerusalem and a number of lawyers wrote histories of the Templar Order. The Priory building of St. John at Clerkenwell, had a more varied history, serving as a tavern and printing office before becoming the home of the revived Order of St. John, but it then also became the venue for its ceremonies and celebrations and its restoration and decoration drew heavily on past history. In addition, enthusiastic antiquarians and archaeologists uncovered remains which were claimed as knights of the Orders and there was lively debate about such identifications in the periodicals of the time. Material remains are therefore a key element of what might be described as the memory jigsaw of the Military Orders in Britain.

Notes

1 See chapter, pp. 17, 23.
2 For a detailed discussion of the crossed-legs effigies, see Oliver Harris, 'Antiquarian Attitudes: Crossed Legs and the Evolution of an Idea', *The Antiquaries Journal* 90 (2010), 416–23.
3 Harris p. 418; Francis Blomefield, *An Essay towards a Topographical History of the County of Norfolk*, 5 vols, vol. 3 (1739–75), p. 416.
4 Mills, 2, p. 8 n.
5 Harris, p. 422.
6 George V. Irving, 'Knights Templar in Scotland', *Notes and Queries 3rd series* 8 (1865), 312.
7 Horace Walpole, *Letters*, XXXVIII, pp. 110–11; XL, pp. 200–2.
8 For the Temple effigies, see also above, pp. 32–3.
9 *The Temple Church in London. History, Architecture, Art.* ed. Robin Griffith-Jones and David Park. (Woodbridge, 2017).
10 Edmund Spenser, *Prothalamion* l. 127, www.poetryfoundation.org, accessed 17 April 2023.
11 Griffith-Jones, "An Enrichment of Cherubims: Sir Christopher Wren's Refurbishment of the Temple Church', in *The Temple Church in London*, 135–75.
12 See Philip J. Lankester, "The Thirteenth-Century Effigies in the Temple Church', in *The Temple Church in London*, pp. 100–3.
13 Robert W. Billings, *Architectural Illustrations and Account of the Temple church* (London, 1838).
14 Charles Knight, *Old England: A Pictorial Museum of Regal, Ecclesiastical, Baronial, Municipal and Popular Antiquities*, 2 vols, vol. 1 (London, 1845–6), pp. 142–6.
15 Phyllis Saunders, *Within the Magic Gateways: A Fairy Story of the Temple* (London, 1919); for the painting by Margaret Kemp-Welch, see www.rct.org.uk, accessed 17 April 2023.
16 *The Intimate Letters of Hester Piozzi and Penelope Pennington 1788–1821*, ed. Oswald G. Knapp (London, 1914), p. 5.

17 Yale Center for British Art, *Whyte Family Correspondence* MSS 19, Box 1, Folder 33.
18 Samuel Lewis, 'Tremerchion' in *A Topographical Dictionary of Wales*, 2 vols (London, 1840) and Kathryn Hurlock, *Wales and the Crusades 1095–1291* (Cardiff, 2011), p. 116.
19 Siberry, *New Crusaders*, pp. 58 and 123.
20 Thackeray, *A Little Dinner at Timmins* ch. 1. The story was first published in instalments in *Punch* between May and July 1848. For Thackeray and the London Library, see Siberry, 'Nineteenth Century Readers', pp. 10–13.
21 See above, p. 12.
22 Thackeray provided illustrations for Addison's *Damascus to Palmyra. A Journey to the East* published in 1838.
23 Scott, *The Antiquary*, ed. David Hewitt (Edinburgh, 1995), p. 168.
24 Gough, *Sepulchral Monuments*, 1, p. 5; James Peller Malcolm, *Londinium Redivivum* (London, 1803), p. 25.
25 See George Godwin, *The Churches of London* (London, 1838), pp. 25–31.
26 *Rosemary Sweet*, '"A Neat structure with Pillars": Changing Perceptions of the Temple Church in the Long Eighteenth Century', *The Temple Church*, p. 193.
27 Richard J. Schoek, 'The Elizabethan Society of Antiquaries and Men of Law', *Notes and Queries* 199 (1954), 417–21.
28 Walford, 'On Cross-Legged Effigies' pp. 49–52. Walford published widely on heraldic matters and was elected an FSA in 1853.
29 Henry Baylis, *The Temple Church and Chapel of St. Ann* (London, 1893).
30 Hugh H.L. Bellot, *The Inner and Middle Temple. Legal, Literary and Historic Associations* (London, 1902).
31 John Yonge Anderson Morshead, *The Templars' Trials* (London 1888).
32 *Saturday Review*, 11 August 1888, p. 191.
33 Chris Miele 'Gothic Sign, Protestant Regalia: Templars, Ecclesiologists and the Round Churches at Cambridge and London', *Architectural History* 53 (2010), p. 198.
34 https://www.rct.ukcollection/811122/the-master-of-the-inn-confers-the-order-of-knighthood-of-don-quixote. The print can also be found in other major collections suggesting that it was widely known and reflects the use of imagery relating to the crusades at the time of the French revolutionary wars. See Siberry, 'Crusading against France, 1789–1815', forthcoming.
35 See www.watercolourworld.com, accessed 17 April 2023.
36 Herman Melville, *Journal of a Visit to London and the Continent 1849–50*, ed. Eleanor M. Metcalf (London, 1949), pp. 24, 98; *Journals*, ed. Howard C. Horsford and Lynn Horton (Chicago, 1989) pp. 16, 281 and 'The Paradise of Bachelors' in *Apple Tree Table and Other Sketches*, ed. Henry Chapin (Princeton, 1922), p. 168.
37 William Whyte, 'Restoration and Recrimination: The Temple Church in the Nineteenth Century', *Temple Church*, pp. 195–211.
38 Review of Addison and Summerly in *Architect, Engineer and Surveyor*, 4 (January 1843), 18–20.
39 *Gentleman's Magazine* n.s. 17 (1842), 654–5.
40 *Gentleman's Magazine* n.s 45, 1 (1856), 406–7.
41 *The Times*, 21 November 1842, p. 5.
42 *Illustrated London News*, 5 November 1842, p. 412.
43 Griffith-Jones, 'The Latter Glory of This House. Some Details of Damage and Repair 1840–1941' in *Temple Church*, p. 219.
44 Sydney Smirke, *The Architecture, Embellishments and Painted Glass of the Temple Church* (London, 1845)
45 John Kenworthy-Browne, 'Plaster Casts from the Crystal Palace Sydenham', *Sculpture Journal* 15 (2006), 173–98.

46 *Punch*, 28 May 1870, p. 216.
47 Inner Temple Archives, BUI/9/2. Inner Temple Hall: Hall Building Committee Minutes. Enclosed correspondence and papers concerning the decoration, windows and bronze figures for the new Hall and rough minutes 1870–77. I am grateful to Celia Pilkington, Inner Temple archivist, for her help on this.
48 Church Monuments Society, *Autumn Newsletter* 37 (2021), pp. 21–2; Richard Knowles, 'Tales of an Arabian Knight: The T.E. Lawrence Effigy', *Church Monuments* 6 (1991), 67–76.
49 *Sermons Preached at the 700th Anniversary of the Consecration of the Temple Church* (London, 1885), pp. 4–5, 13–14, 20.
50 See Horswell, pp. 41–2.
51 Ainger also published a history of the Temple with 12 illustrative etchings.
52 *700th Anniversary Service*, pp. 29, 49, 51–2, 66, 74, 76–8.
53 *The Times*, 2 and 9 March 1885, pp. 10 and 7 respectively.
54 'The Seventh Centenary of the Temple Church', *Saturday Review*, 7 March 1885, pp. 687–9.
55 See David Lewer and Robert Dark, *The Temple Church in London* (London, 1997), pp. 30–32.
56 *The Times*, 15 December 1917, p. 7.
57 *Jerusalem. A Sermon preached in Commemoration of the Capture of Jerusalem on Sunday December 16th at the Temple church by the Revd. E. W. Barnes Master of the Temple*. London 1918. I am grateful to Barnaby Bryan, Archivist of the Middle Temple, for providing me with a copy of the sermon.
58 *Saturday Review*, 2 Feburary 1918, p. 91.
59 Charles Darling, *Inner Templars Who Volunteered and Served in the Great War* (1917).
60 Griffith-Jones, 'The Latter Glory of This House', *Temple Church*, p. 218 and Image 106.
61 https://www.british-history.ac.uk/survey-london/vol46/pp.142-163, accessed 28 July 2023.
62 *A Concise History of the Ancient and Illustrious Order of the Knights Hospitallers of St. John of Jerusalem, Rhodes and Malta* (London, 1834). Till dedicates his work to the knights and describes himself as their faithful friend and companion. Copies survive in the collection of Chetham's Library in Manchester and the Order of St. John Museum.
63 Nigel Hankin, 'Acquiring Heritage: The Order of St. John and the Accumulation of Its Past (1858–1931)' in *Modern Memory*, pp. 43–62. See also below, pp. 71–2.
64 Catherine. E. Hundley, 'The English Round Church Movement' in *Tomb and Temple. Re-Imagining the Sacred Buildings of Jerusalem* (Woodbridge, 2018), pp. 368–9.
65 John Britton, *The Architecture and Antiquities of Britain*, 5 vols (London, 1807–26), vol. 1, pp. v–vi and Plates xiv, xvii, xviii and xix.
66 See Christopher Miele, 'Gothic Sign and the Round Churches at Cambridge and London' and Revd. J. Charles Cox and Revd. R.M. Serjeantson, *A History of the Church of the Holy Sepulchre, Northampton* (Northampton, 1897).
67 William Wallen, *The History and Antiquities of the Round Church at Little Maplestead Essex* (London, 1836).
68 Christopher Webster, 'An Alternative to Ecclesiology: William Wallen (1807–53)', *Ecclesiology Today* 42 (2010), 9–28.
69 Wallen, p. 159.
70 *The Round Church of Little Maplestead* (London, 1851).
71 *Athenaeum*, 23 July 1836, pp. 517–18.
72 Frederick W. Fairholt, *Costume in England* (London, 1846), pp. 149–51; Samuel Meyrick, *A Critical Inquiry into Ancient Armour as It Existed in Europe*, 3 vols.

(London, 1824); Charles Hamilton Smith, *Selections of the Ancient Costume of Great Britain and Ireland from the 7th Century to the 16th Century* (London, 1814). Smith's drawings of members of the military orders are now in the collection of the Houghton Library, Harvard, USA.

73 *History of Temple Church* (Bodmin, 1883).

74 See Simon Brighton, *In Search of the Knights Templar* (London, 2008), pp. 142–7. *The Church of St Mary the Virgin Temple Balsall. Visitor Guide* (2004).

75 https://warwickshirechurches.weebly.com>temple-grafton-st-andrew.html, accessed 17 April 2023.

76 Brighton, pp. 188–92.

77 See Martin Crampin, *Stained Glass in Wales* (Llandysul, 2014), pp. 198–9.

78 The answer probably lies in the A.L. Moore archive held by the Victoria and Albert Museum, but this is not accessible until 2025. See also Siberry, 'Memorials to Crusaders', p. 190.

79 William Rees, *A History of the Order of St. John of Jerusalem in Wales* (Cardiff, 1947).

80 Siberry, 'Memorials to Crusaders', p. 186.

81 Richard Hollins Murray, *Dinmore Manor* (1936).

82 *Harewood Park. England's Lost Country Houses*, http://www.lostheritage.org.uk/houses/lj_herefordshire_harewoodpark.html, accessed 20 July 2023.

83 *Receipted bill for work in the church, including making a box and vault "for the Knight Templars Bones" 188*, Dorset archives PE-SKG/CW/2/1. A copy of the notes is also in the Dorset Archives, PE-SKG/AQ/1.

84 John Hutchins, *The History and Antiquities of the County of Dorset*, 2nd ed (1813) I, p. 252.

85 Harris, pp. 420–1.

86 See Thomas H. Fosbroke, 'Rothley. The Preceptory', *Transactions of the Leicestershire Archaeological and Historical Society* 12 (1922), pp. 39–40.

87 Clarke, 'The Babingtons, Knights of St. John', 219–30.

88 Nicholls, p. 112.

89 Rothley Court Hotel. https://www.greenkinginns.co.uk/hotel>rothleycourt, accessed 17 April 2023.

90 Thomas Gisborne, *Rothley Temple; A Poem in Three Cantos* (London, 1815).

91 *Gentleman's Magazine* 59 (1) (1789) 337–8. See also p. 496.

92 Philip Morant, *The History and Antiquities of the County of Essex*, II, p. 30 (London, 1768). The 'tradition' mentioned is a reference to Weaver's *Funeral Monuments*. For the examination of the remains of the last Grand Prior of England, Sir William Weston, see below, p. 72.

93 William H. St. John Hope, 'The Round Church of the Knights Templar at Temple Bruer Lincolnshire', *Archaeologia* 61 (1905), 177–98.

94 Lizzie Swarbrick, 'Templar Pseudo History, Symbology and the Far-Right' in *The Modern Memory of the Military-Religious Orders*, pp. 21–42.

3　Reinventing knights

Reinventing knights

In the nineteenth century, various attempts were made in Britain to revive (or reinvent) the English langue of the Order of St. John and the Templars. This chapter will look at the history of the Orders in this period and some of the individuals involved. It will also, building on the analysis of the Orders' historiography, reading, reception and material memory discussed in Chapters 1 and 2, look at the way in which the Orders used their history to underpin their contemporary work and some of the schemes put forward to re-establish the Orders in the Middle East.

Order of St. John after dissolution and Napoleon

The British estates of the Order were confiscated by King Henry VIII in 1540 and the Order dissolved. By 1542, there were only three knights remaining in Malta as active members of the English langue.[1] Some gentlemen volunteers from Britain and Ireland took part in the defence of Malta in 1565, but the only English knight to fight in the siege, Oliver Starkey, Secretary to Grand Master La Valette, died in 1588. Efforts thereafter to revive the English langue in its old form failed and in 1782 it was combined with the newly formed Bavarian langue, as the Anglo Bavarian langue.

The Irish baronet, Sir Joshua Colles Meredyth was received into the Order in early 1798 but, after the fall of Malta to Napoleon that summer, the Grand Master Ferdinand von Hompesch and his knights were expelled from the island. Von Hompesch found refuge in Trieste and in November 1798, Tsar Paul of Russia, who had always been fascinated by the knights and was a keen reader of Vertot, was elected Grand Master.[2] The following decades were difficult times for the Order, with langues abolished or acting independently and no permanent base. In its 1805 review of a history of the Order by Count Boisgelin, the *Edinburgh Review* commented:

> It is certainly a most extraordinary fact, that, at the end of the eighteenth century there should still exist a society of men, whose members, uniting

DOI: 10.4324/9781003177234-4

the most discordant characters, professed at once to adopt the austerities of a religious order, and to wage perpetual war with the enemies of the Christian faith. Yet such was the Order of St. John of Jerusalem, which, of all the institutions to which the crusades have given rise, exhibited the most heterogeneous mixture of Christian humility and temporal pride, the most singular attempt to reconcile the possession of rich benefices and luxurious indulgences, with vows of poverty and professions of self denial.[3]

And in a novel, entitled *Emily: A Moral Tale*, the Revd. Henry Kett described one of his characters, Baron Belfield, a former member of the Order, who celebrated its past achievements, but was 'deeply sensible of the unworthiness of many of its modern members' who had failed to defend Malta against Napoleon.[4]

These two examples give a sense of the environment in which attempts to revive the Order in Britain took place. By 1834, however, the catholic Sovereign Order of Malta was able to establish its headquarters in Rome, where they remain to the present day and the British Association of the Sovereign Order was founded in 1875.

The backcloth to such debates was of course British involvement in Malta, which was confirmed as a crown colony by the Treaty of Paris in 1814 and served as a key military base. This interplay between the ambitions of the Sovereign Order and British politics in the Mediterranean in the nineteenth century is another area meriting further archival research.

The Sovereign Order of Malta in Britain

A small number of British Roman Catholics were admitted as members of the Sovereign Order in the first half of the nineteenth century. John Taaffe, a member of a family from County Louth in Ireland long associated with the Military Orders, and historian of the Order of St. John, was made a knight in 1836 and successfully petitioned King William IV to allow him to wear the regalia of the order at Windsor Castle in the same year, although this was normally forbidden because it was regarded as a foreign order.[5] The historian of the crusades, Charles Mills was also elected a knight in recognition of his 'allusions to that fraternity' shortly before his death in 1826.[6] Nevertheless, numbers remained few in the 1830s and 1840s, although there were more elections in the following two decades.

In 1858 two other British knights, the antiquary John James Watts and the MP and lawyer Sir George Bowyer, were appointed to the Order.[7] Their personal histories provide an insight into the Order at this time and the discussions which ultimately led to the foundation of the British Association of the Sovereign Order of Malta (BASOM), as well as the early troubled history of the British Order of St. John.

John James Watts

Watts was a keen historian and genealogist of the Order. His family home was Hawkesdale Hall, Cumberland, but he spent much of his life outside England and by the late 1850s, he was living in Malta, where he became involved, as will be discussed later, in attempts to revive English langue. His detailed studies of the pedigrees and heraldry of Knights of Malta have been preserved in the archives of the Society of Antiquaries in London and are an important source for the early membership of both Orders.[8] He also wrote notes on the history of both the Knights of St. John and the Templars.

George Bowyer

George Bowyer had converted to Catholicism in 1850 and became a knight of the Order in 1858.[9] In 1850, Pope Pius IX had announced the restoration of the Roman Catholic hierarchy in England and the appointment of Nicholas Wiseman as Archbishop of Westminster, and this attracted significant opposition and aroused strong anti-catholic feeling.[10] Against this background, Bowyer's membership of the Order prompted some criticism. While the *Times* simply reported the event,[11] the popular *Saturday Review* declared, in a satirical article entitled *The revival of Chivalry*:

> The age or chivalry has not passed away. It is a satisfaction when there are many more chevaliers d'industrie than Bayards in the world, to know that a genuine live Hospitaller is among us.

The author lamented the lack of ceremony:

> Simply to be called a Hospitaller and to go about in society with an ordinary black hat and varnished boots, with only the proud internal consciousness that you are a spiritual and chivalrous descendant of Raymond du Puy, and that in an unbroken line you trace your military ancestry up to the twelfth century would not satisfy half so much as the substantial and tangible installation.

Satirical pen firmly poised, the article went on to question whether, if Bowyer 'had taken the cross and lance a few years ago, the European [Crimean] War about the Holy Places might not have been prevented', and queried whether there was some conspiracy to occupy Malta again.[12]

The same publication also questioned the value of the Order in a combined review of histories by Baron Elize de Montagnac and Whitworth Porter:[13]

> Few people are aware that the Knights of St. John still exist and it would be more honourable for the Order if it did not exist…the days of its greatness

and its usefulness have passed away, and all that was left for it was to end gloriously...what inducement there can be nowadays to lead anybody to become a knight of St. John is something quite beyond our powers of guessing.[14]

British association of the Order of Malta

The British Association of the Catholic Sovereign Military and Hospitaller Order of St. John of Jerusalem (commonly now known as the Sovereign Military Order of Malta) (BASOM), was eventually founded in December 1875 and held its first General Assembly on 24 May 1876. The first President of the British Association was the Irish peer, the 7th Earl of Granard, who held this office until his death in 1889. All members of the Sovereign Order residing in the United Kingdom had been invited to attend and he reported that 26 had signified their support, although Watts declined to do so.

The General Assembly took place in the church of St. John of Jerusalem, in the hospital of St. John and St. Elizabeth, in Great Ormond Street, London, which had been established in 1856 and was staffed by the Sisters of Mercy, nuns who had worked with Florence Nightingale during the Crimean War. Bowyer was a key figure in its development and funded the building of the church, designed by the leading catholic architect George Goldie, which prominently displayed the Maltese cross.[15] The President formally thanked Bowyer for his generosity and 'devoted zeal for the honour of the Order'. In his response, he reflected on the difficulties and jealousies aroused by the establishment of the Association and hoped that 'new men, unconnected with former events and differences' could now hold its principal offices and take forward its work. In 1881, the Prince of Wales was made a Bailiff Grand Cross of the Order.[16]

The BASOM still has its headquarters in London and is active in medical and humanitarian charitable work.

Reviving the English langue

Revival and rejection

The story of attempts to establish and obtain recognition for an English langue in the first half of the nineteenth century and the colourful individuals who joined it has already been told by Jonathan Riley- Smith.[17] It began, against the background of efforts to raise funds for the Greek revolt against the Ottoman empire and the possible reconquest of Rhodes as a home for the displaced Order. In 1826, emissaries from the independent French langue, under the so-called Marquis Pierre Hippolyte de Sainte-Croix-Molay, opened negotiations with Donald Currie, a Scot living in London, to raise £240,000 by private subscription, that would be used to employ men and buy arms for a Mediterranean expedition. Currie recruited a number of individuals and was authorised to form a committee to revive the English langue. By the mid-1830s, there were in fact two English langues – one recognised by the French under Count Alexander Mortara and the other, comprising Currie and individuals such as Revd. Robert Peat, the rector of New Brentford in Middlesex and a former chaplain of George IV.

Peat was elected Prior of the revived English langue in 1831 and by the time of his death in 1837, only his langue remained. In February 1834, Peat took an oath before the Court of the King's Bench in London and did:

> then and there openly qualify himself before the Lord Chief Justice of England, Sir Thomas Denham, to hold, exercise and discharge the office of Prior of the langue of England under the charter of King Philip and Queen Mary.[18]

In 1837, two members of the langue, William Crawford and Robert Lucas Pearsall, were sent to France and Germany to make contact with knights there. Approaches were also made to George III's son, the Duke of Sussex and other members of the royal family to provide royal endorsement and prestige, but they declined. Intriguingly, the subject chosen for the Oxford Newdigate poetry prize in 1836, won by Frederick Faber, was the Knights of St. John, which may reflect wider interest in the subject.[19]

Peat was succeeded by another Scot, Richard Broun, who was Registrar and Grand Secretary until his death in 1858. Interest in establishing an English langue waxed and waned in the 1840s,[20] but discussions included ambitious plans for the Christian reoccupation of the Holy Land. Sir William Hillary, now better known as a founder of the Royal National Lifeboat Institution, had visited Malta in 1797, just before the Napoleonic invasion, and on 5 December 1840, inspired by news of the capture of Acre, he wrote to Richard Broun proposing a role for the Order:

> Let then the Order of St. John of Jerusalem be patronised and supported by all the Christian powers and remodelled where necessary and practicable, to suit the occasion and let the paschalics of Gaza and Acre be placed under their sovereign rule paying only stipulated annual revenue to the Sultan; the perpetual neutrality and possession to be guaranteed to the Order, both by Christian and Mohammedan powers.

Hillary's proposal was discussed at the Chapter of Council meeting and a pamphlet *Suggestions for the Christian Occupation of the Holy Land as a Sovereign State by the Order of St. John of Jerusalem* was printed in London in 1841 and reprinted in newspapers such as the *Morning Herald*. The proposal, however, came to nothing and Hillary died in 1847.[21]

Interest in the langue revived in the aftermath of the Crimean War, but a key issue was the status and independence of a langue whose members were Protestant. John Taaffe had lamented the absence of a recognised English Langue and drew attention to the noble contribution of English knights in his history of the Order of St. John published in 1852, but he recognised the practical difficulty:

> We may regret the severity which bade the noble English language cease existing-and fearlessly do we add the sooner it is restored the better, but first by inevitable relation to the Order in which it had the honour of belonging, and without which it can no more live than the branch without the trunk.[22]

In 1857, it was decided to use Watts, then resident in Malta, as an intermediary with the Grand Magistry in Rome. He reported back to Broun and the signals were positive initially. At the Chapter General held in Clerkenwell on St. John's Day, 24 June 1858, Broun declared:

> Since the formal revival of our langue nearly 30 years have passed over our heads, and within that period it has enrolled a chivalry of about 140 members (including two British monarchs) of whom upwards of 100 are now alive. Consolidated therefore, by progression of time, and already both respectable and strong in point of numbers and social influence, the period has now assuredly arrived-if indeed the Order in British soil is ever destined again to play a conspicuous part as an institute of utility here and throughout the Christian world-for the langue to be up and vigorously take the field.

Broun went on to suggest that the Order should reoccupy the island of Rhodes as the 'chief lieu for the Order in the Levant' and a 'crusade' of Christian colonisation and, as already noted, in 1856 he produced a *Synoptical Sketch* of the Order for circulation to members of the langue.[23]

The English catholic knights, Edmund Waterton and George Bowyer were tasked to negotiate the restoration of a Grand Priory of England and initial indications seemed positive. The Magisterial Secretary, the Count of Gozze, wrote in July 1858:

> I see in its arrangement all the characteristics of moderation, of justice, of loyalty, and of prudence, which the Council of London desires to bring to the settlement. Speaking for myself, and without prejudicing the decision of the Council of the Order at Rome, I think I may here enunciate my firm conviction that this article contains nothing which, after being clearly defined and well leavened, may not be frankly accepted by the Order.[24]

In fact, Waterton and Bower dismissed the English langue as 'humbug' and described some of its leading members as 'imposters' and 'swindlers'. On 20 December 1858, the Sovereign Order broke any remaining links with the English Order stating unequivocally that it:

> had never been in any organic connection with the above society, either at the origin of the said society, or at any later period.

In order to leave no room for doubt, copies of this protest were sent to the Prince Consort (a Knight Grand Cross of the Sovereign Order since 1839), the Lord Chamberlain, the Home Secretary and the College of Arms.[25]

In his history published in 1858, Whitworth Porter wrote of the current situation:

> Grave doubts exist as to the legitimacy of this revived Branch of the English language. The authorities in supreme governance over the Order in Rome deny its validity and refuse to recognise it as an integral branch of the Venerable Order of St. John. It would be well, therefore, if such steps could be taken as should decide the question and remove the uncertainty which at present exists on the matter.

The sensitivities are highlighted in correspondence, preserved in the British Association archives, between Bowyer, Waterton and Watts about the publication of Porter's history. The knights were anxious that Porter should describe the attempts to revive the langue 'correctly' and in October 1858, Watts told Waterton that he had given Porter the whole story 'to his amusement and astonishment'. In November 1858, Porter responded:

> I have steered a middle course touching the spurious English branch. My publishers anxious not to give offence.

Correspondence between Watts and Bowyer indicates that they found the resulting publication disappointing. Bowyer wrote that he was, 'disgusted with Porter's treatment of the pseudo langue. Not strong enough'.

He went on to publish a highly critical review in the *Dublin Review* in 1859, in which he challenged the ability of a Protestant to write effectively about a Catholic order:

> The Major has executed his task with industry and ability. But it was not possible for a Protestant to write anything deserving the name of a history of an institution so Catholic as a religious order. He could not understand the spirit, nor its fundamental principles, nor the characters of its heroes... nor account for its vitality or its greatness. His book, therefore, in two large volumes, is nothing but a dry compilation of facts, a lifeless chronicle of

events…It is very much like a regimental history. It is interspersed with the usual protestant common places.

And he added, referring to the attempts to revive the English langue, that Porter was incapable of discriminating between truth and error.[26] Some of Bowyer's fellow knights thought that his views had been 'tactlessly expressed', but the strong language used provides further evidence of the challenge facing those who sought to revive the Order in Britain.[27]

Patient consolidation

Against this background and after the debacle of 1858, the 1860s and 1870s were a period of review and consolidation, although considerable challenges remained. The key figures were the Duke of Manchester, who served as Prior from 1861 to 1888; Sir Edmund Lechmere (a Conservative MP and Secretary General 1868–90) and Sir John Furley, a humanitarian who worked to improve medical care in peace and wartime.

In his history of the Order published in 1863, James Bryans wrote of its present and future prospects:

> The knights of the langue of England, who have laboured so long, so zealously and disinterestedly to promote its cause, only desire to prove by acts and deeds of a meritorious description, that they do not assert their place as an order of chivalry without aspiring to reoccupy their ancient status in such a manner as shall make their institution worthy of their proud historical reminiscences.[28]

Evidence of the continuing controversy can, however, be found in a lengthy correspondence published in the periodical *Notes and Queries*, which described itself as a medium of intercommunication for literary men, readers, writers, collectors and librarians. In 1860, a correspondent, who styled himself *Constant Reader*, had asked where he could find authentic information about the present state and position of the English langue. John Woodward, who wrote regularly on the various historical issues, responded:

> The best book on the present condition of the English langue…is the Synoptical Sketch of the Order printed a few years ago; but I fear your correspondent will find difficulty in procuring it, except from a member of the Order for which it was printed.

He offered instead his copy of the general ordinances of the Langue.[29]

Constant Reader asked his question again in 1863 and this time he prompted not only some suggestions about links between the Order, the Knights Templar and Freemasons, but also a detailed refutation of the legitimacy of the revived langue by, among others, George Bowyer. A writer using the name *Historicus* declared:

> The "Articles of Convention" by which the "English langue" claims to be revived, are not worth the paper on which they are written. And noone who reads the Synoptical Sketch and tests it by its own statements and by collateral evidence, as I have done, can fail to come to the same conclusion.

He concluded that:

> it is quite evident that the aforesaid institution which calls itself the "Venerable English Langue of the Sovereign Order of St. John of Jerusalem" has not the slightest right either legal or moral to assume that title and designation, or to represent itself as being what, from its official testimony and that of the Order of St. John it is not.[30]

John James Watts also wrote to the periodical to underline the claims of the Sovereign Order as 'the true and glorious relic' and its Grand Master as the true heir of his predecessors, Pierre d'Aubusson and Jean de la Valette. The debate was not, however, completely one-sided. In May 1863, Whitworth Porter, whose comments on the langue had been criticised by *Historicus*, sought to refute the latter's arguments point by point and another writer styled *Antiquarius* also supported the legitimacy of the English Order.[31]

The subject was also discussed in the popular *Gentleman's Magazine* in May 1867. Here a writer, styled JUD, advocated the cause of the Order with a renewed charitable purpose:

> Why, in this age of peculiar demand for the most active exertions of individuals and societies for the succour and relief of millions of our fellow creatures...should not the old and time-honoured brotherhood of the Knights of St. John claim a new stage for the exercise of their high mission of utility and benevolence...We fear that it is but imperfectly known that there exists in England an association of distinguished persons, with the Duke of Manchester at their head, who are devotedly attached to the objects thus set forth.

The article went on to support ambitions of territorial expansion:

> who would not delight to see the white cross of the ancient soldiery of St. John once more wave above the reconsecrated domes and towers of its former home in Jerusalem...and a noble army of Christian warriors... perform a glorious and enduring service-carrying freedom and civilisation to those unhappy races who are now immersed in the direst poverty and most galling degradation.[32]

In the Preface to his 1869 history, Robert Bigsby, a Knight of the English langue since 1835, described the:

> period of the revival of…the venerable Langue of England, which has been the subject of so many vituperative attacks from a body of ultramontane Romanists opposed to its reconstruction on a Protestant basis.

Bigsby's history also reprinted newspaper and journal reports of the Order's activities, such as the *Daily Telegraph's* report of the proceedings of the 1868 Chapter General.[33]

Key foundations

Better times came in the 1870s. In 1870, Lechmere wrote to the Vice Chancellor of the Sovereign Order seeking 'to let all bygones remain in the shadows of the past', explaining the work of the Order in England and offering:

> to unite and work with other branches of the order in that great cause of humanity, which as ever distinguished one of the brightest ornaments of the chivalry of Europe.[34]

The response made clear that the Order's Protestantism remained the obstacle and by 1871, a new constitution for the British Order of St. John had been established and Lechmere and others began to lay the key foundations for the future.

Richard Woof and setting the record straight

The Archives of the Order at Clerkenwell contain letters from this era which merit further detailed study. For example, Richard Woof (also sometimes known by the family name Woolfe), Registrar of the Order and his fellow member, later Librarian of the Order, Colonel Hunter Weston, discussed some of the hostages to fortune which critics might uncover in the Order's history. Woof had already published *A Sketch of the Knights Templars and the Knights Hospitallers of St. John of Jerusalem* in 1865 and in 1872, he sought to set out the facts behind the troubled history of the revived English langue in *A brief narrative of circumstances attending the revival and progress of the English langue of the Order of St. John of Jerusalem*. Woof sent his draft text to a number of fellow members of the Order for comment and in August 1872, Whitworth Porter wrote from Malta:

> You have put forward a very powerful defence and have grasped the true spirit of our cause…I can only congratulate the Order upon having found

a member so well qualified to put together the real facts of the case upon which we found our claims to legitimacy.

It was also endorsed by the November 1872 Chapter General, although never published under Woof's name.
Woof argued:

> That the revival of the Order in England was conducted and accomplished in the most honourable spirit and with the highest intentions, there is no room for doubt. The few English gentlemen whose interest was enlisted in the revival...were men of the highest character, distinguished by superior learning and attainments and to whom no breath of suspicion can attach.

He set out the chronology of events, quoting from original documents and noted that opposition had not only come from the Order at Rome, but also, perhaps referring to the exchanges in *Notes and Queries*:

> Individual (anonymous) correspondents of periodicals, some of whom were not members of the Order; others belonging to then Roman Catholic branch. The attacks of these gentlemen have been made in a hostile and bitter spirit which it is not intended to imitate here.[35]

As well as his work for the Order, Woof was also a historian of his home county of Worcestershire and after his death in 1877, his memorial tablet in Worcester cathedral (Figure 3.1) described his varied interests and contribution as follows:

> Fellow of the Society of Antiquaries, Registrar of the English langue of the Order of St. John of Jerusalem and for many years Town Clerk and Magistrates clerk of this city.

In 1905, he was one of ten deceased members of the Order to be honoured with a brass plaque in the crypt at Clerkenwell.

As part of setting the record straight, in 1878 the Order published *A Brief Note of its Foundation and Constitution and its Objects in England*, which had been the subject of much correspondence and concerns between key founding members. It noted that, at the 1826 Chapter General, the 'resuscitation of the Order in England was resolved' and the significance of Sir Robert Peat's oath before the Court of King's Bench, taken at the instigation of Sir Lancelot Shadwell, the Vice Chancellor of England:

> What may have induced the Vice Chancellor to suggest this procedure is now unknown, but it was certainly a most formal mode of giving publicity to the fact that the Order had been revived in England.

Figure 3.1 Memorial to Richard Woof, Worcester Cathedral. Author's photo.

There was optimism for the future, both in terms of work to be done and growing membership.

It now remains to be stated what the English branch of the Order has ef-
fected since its revival and to point out the wide field of usefulness which
lies before it…With ever increasing accession to its roll of persons of rank
and influence, the Order of St. John in England is advancing in its power

and means of doing good, and its unobtrusive and persevering efforts in the cause of humanity, as well as its opportunities of applying those efforts, are happily becoming enlarged.[36]

Clerkenwell

As another literal building block for the future, in 1873 the freehold of the dilapidated medieval gatehouse of the Hospitallers in Clerkenwell was purchased by Lechmere, who in so doing may have outbid the Sovereign Order.[37] Lechmere subsequently leased part of the building to the Order of St. John, which obtained the freehold in 1887. And, as practical evidence of its charitable aims, in 1878, the St. John Ambulance Association (SJAA) was formed and in 1882, the Eye Hospital in Jerusalem was established.

Caring for the sick

The important link made between the care of the sick and wounded during the crusades and the SJAA, treating casualties of war, modern industry and transport, was reflected in the language used. In 1884, Surgeon Major George Hutton told those receiving certificates in Wigan that they were' embracing all that was noble in the traditions handed down to them by the old Knights of St. John of Jerusalem' and he launched a series of 'ambulance crusades'.[38] And in 1887, Lady Knightley told an ambulance gathering at Northampton:

> They in this nineteenth century were carrying on in the same spirit the work which was begun some 800 years ago…The Order had passed through many vicissitudes and its history was perhaps not altogether one to look back upon as satisfactory, but she believed many great and noble acts had been carried out under its auspices and it seemed to her a very beautiful thought that in the nineteenth century they were carrying out the original Christian idea of helping pilgrims who fell by the way.[39]

The key figure in the establishment and success of the Ambulance Association, Sir John Furley, had attended the Geneva conference of Red Cross societies in 1869 and had firsthand experience of the challenges of treating battlefield casualties from the 1870 siege of Paris and many members of the Ambulance Association served as medical orderlies in the Boer War.[40] The Order's contribution during the First World War was also justly praised and inspired a number of publications. An illustration, which appeared in *Punch* in 1914 entitled The Order of St. John 1099–1914, showed a ghostly knight observing members of St. John's Ambulance tending to a soldier on the battlefield.[41] In parallel, the Order extended its global reach throughout the British Empire.[42]

Royal recognition

With the foundations of the modern Order in place and proof of the contribution it had made and could make to British life, came royal recognition. In 1888, Queen Victoria approved a royal charter for the Grand Priory of the Order of the Hospital of St. John of Jerusalem in England and in August that year, the Prince of Wales, who in his youth had visited some of the sites associated with the crusades,[43] was installed as Grand Prior. The *Times* reported the ceremony, commenting on the Order's work and its proud history:

> The Order has for many years been known to the public as a philanthropic body of high standing, and more especially during the last few years, from the extensive operations of its ambulance department, more familiarly known as St. John's Ambulance. The whole scheme of its operations, indeed is, as far as possible, by adaptation to the requirements of modern times, the perpetuation of the Hospitaller work of the famous Order of Saint John of Jerusalem which in the Middle Ages was the most striking and practical order of chivalry.[44]

The article listed the many members of the royal family who had attended the ceremony and were themselves members of the Order. And, on 24 June 1893, the feast day of St. John the Baptist, the Prince of Wales opened the newly restored St. John's Gate in Clerkenwell.

Not all critics, however, had been silenced. A letter to *The Times*, published on 6 April 1888, stated that the claims of the Order were 'based on garbled documents and on statements that are directly contrary to fact',[45] and the General Assembly of the BASOM that year registered its protest.[46]

The Order's royal patronage remained important. In 1897, Queen Victoria's Diamond Jubilee was marked by the launch of a charitable appeal and *Punch* published a cartoon showing the Prince of Wales dressed as a knight on horseback entitled as 'Our new knight hospitaller'. He carried a banner with the words Loyalty and Charity and was preceded by a figure of charity with a collection box bearing the words Jubilee Hospital Fund. An accompanying poem declared:

> Gifts to charity the cause
> Of the poor our Prince well pleadeth
> Not mere salvoes of applause
> Our Knight-Hospitaller needeth.
> Largess, largess! Tis his claim
> Urged with simple kindly clarity
> In the loved and honoured name
> Of our Queen and gentle charity[47]

In the same year, the Prince of Wales, also of course a Bailiff Grand Cross of the Sovereign Order and said to have a 'longstanding affection for the Order of St. John',[48] wore the costume of Grand Prior of the Order at the Duchess of Devonshire's fancy dress ball. The account of the ball described his attire as follows:

> Stout but dignified, he looked most picturesque in his Elizabethan dress of a doublet of black embroidered in steel and jet, with trunks of grey silk slashed with black velvet straps wrought with steel. He wore a high hat trimmed with white plumes and high black turreted boots with large silver spurs. On his doublet he had a diamond Maltese cross, with the genuine Order of St. John of Jerusalem of Malta.[49]

Fancy dress balls and events were popular in the latter half of the nineteenth century and there were even books describing costumes for various 'roles', including a Knight St. John.[50]

Celebrating past history

The Order's desire to celebrate and remind others of its history was clear in the restoration and interior decoration of St. John's Gate.[51] The restoration in the 1890s and early 1900s was led by the architect John Oldrid Scott, who had also restored the Holy Sepulchre church in Northampton. Members of the Order collected and contributed items from Malta and Rhodes, from books to medals and cannon balls, and paintings of Grand Masters and later Priors still decorate the walls of the Chapter Hall, along with shields of members. As Nigel Hankin has noted:

> Collecting books, objects and even buildings associated with the history of the Hospitallers helped reassure the members of the legitimacy of their claim to be 'an ancient and venerable society' constructing a synthetic memory in material form of an imagined collective past.[52]

A poem written in 1881 by John H. Easterbrook, entitled *A Haunted House*, celebrated the history of the site:

> And from these time worn walls which saw your banner
> When first its cross of Mercy was displayed
> Now, in these later days, a knightly order
> Arms for a new crusade:
> The world their battlefield-the work you left them
> To aid the sick and suffering-yet goes on,
> And in a holy warfare still is famous
> The old gate of St. John[53]

The church of St. John became the Grand Priory church and Lechmere was once again key to its acquisition and the transfer of the advowson to the Order in 1909. Oldrid Scott was also involved with its restoration and the annual St. John's service was held there from 1895. The restored church reopened on 21 May 1901, with a thanksgiving service led by the Archdeacon of London, who:

> Sketched a history of the church and the Order of St. John and expressed the hope that the work of restoration might be a means of perpetuating to future generations the spirit of religion and charity which had Inspired the founders of that ancient edifice.

The Chancellor of the Order, Earl Egerton of Tatton, similarly spoke of the building's great antiquity and interesting associations.[54] In June 1902, the Prince of Wales visited the church to unveil a memorial to members of the Order who had died on service in South Africa.[55]

As with St. John's Gate, it was important for the church to have and display material items recalling the Order's history. These included the effigy of the last English Grand Prior, Sir William Weston, who had fought in the 1522 siege of Rhodes and captained the ship that carried the Grand Master and his knights to Malta. His remains had been examined in the 1780s, when St. James's Clerkenwell was demolished and the restoration of the monument in the rebuilt church was paid for by a modern knight, Colonel Hunter Weston, who claimed descent from Sir William. It was then transferred to St. John's in 1931.[56] The stained glass also drew on the Order's history. The widow of a Knight of St. John, Colonel John Man Stuart, commissioned the designer Archibald Nicholson to produce a window for the East end of the church. This was later moved to the crypt and includes an image of Raymond de Puy and coats of arms of English knights and priors.[57]

Service to mark the capture of Jerusalem in 1917

Reference has already been made to the services in the Temple church marking the capture of Jerusalem in December 1917 and the Order of St. John gathered at the Grand Priory church for the same purpose in January 1918. The *St. John Ambulance Gazette* reported:

> There have been many services of thanksgiving for this thrilling feat of British arms, but to this particular service very special solemnity and significance are attached in view of the Order's age-long connection with Jerusalem, of the fact that its history is inseparably bound with the Holy City and that it bears its name.[58]

A procession of knights walked from St. John's Gate to the church and the service was taken by the Prelate of the Order, the Archbishop of York. In his sermon, the Archbishop recalled the deeds of the medieval knights and praised the restored English branch which had proved 'its faithfulness to the old ideals and traditions in the hospital of St. John'. He also drew parallels between those who had gone on crusade and soldiers fighting in the First World War in Jerusalem:

> The City was won, not by hosts of knights with waving pennants and shining armour, but by plain citizens in arms, our brothers taken from the fields and the factories of England and the plains and cities of the British dominions beyond the seas. Their memories of the Holy Places may have been faint and few, recalling distant days in our English schools, but, however unconsciously, they too, like the crusaders, were giving proof of their loyalty to a high ideal.

He added that it was 917 years since the Order had founded its hospital in Jerusalem and 730 years since Jerusalem was lost to Saladin and that a new era had now dawned for the city.[59]

The service was repeated at the newly dedicated chapel of the St. John Ambulance Brigade hospital at Etaples in Northern France. On a visit to Jerusalem in March 1918, the Duke of Connaught, uncle of King George V and Grand Prior, also invested Sir Edmund Allenby with the cross of the Order.[60]

A modern pilgrimage: 1926

The link made between the Order's past and present was very clear in the pilgrimage organised in March 1926:

> The first occasion of an official visit of one of the Tongues of the Order to the scenes of its ancient activities since its evacuation, firstly of Palestine in 1291, secondly of Rhodes in 1523 and thirdly of Malta in 1798.[61]

The original plan had been to visit the Eye Hospital in Jerusalem, but it developed as an opportunity 'to bring home to our members and workers the close connection between that heritage and the present day work'. The end result was a four week journey starting in London and travelling to Venice, where the participants boarded the steamship Asia, which flew the flag of the Order for the first time in the Mediterranean since 1798, for the voyage to the Holy Land, Cyprus, Rhodes and Malta. Over 100 members of the Order joined the pilgrimage and, suitably robed, took part in investitures, processions and services. En route, they listened to lectures on the history of the crusades and in Jerusalem they were shown the alleged sword and spurs of

Figure 3.2 The Pilgrimage of 1926. The Sub-Prior Investing the Governor of Malta with the Insignia of the Order of St. John in the Throne-Room of the Grand Master's Palace at Valletta. Edward Caruana Dingli, 1927. © Museum of the Order of St. John/Bridgeman Images.

Godfrey of Bouillon.[62] Press reports, in national and regional newspapers throughout Britain, described them as modern crusaders and the special correspondent from the *Daily News*, William M. Duckworth, who filed regular reports, wrote:

> Hardly any of us had imagined it possible to organise a twentieth century crusade with real knights wearing black mantles and carrying their Sword of State and other insignia with which they intend to revive the medieval panoply of their venerable order…We do not intend to march or ride on horse or palfrey through the windswept wastes of Asia minor. We come with passports instead of swords, but with the dauntless spirit of healing brotherhood that has made the Order of St. John of Jerusalem the most honoured of all Orders of knighthood.[63]

One of the key organisers was Harry Pirie-Gordon, a Knight of Grace of the Order and enthusiastic historian of the crusades, who as a young man had founded his own Order of chivalry based on the rules of the Order of St. John.[64] A specially commissioned set of five tiles was produced as a souvenir, depicting the arms of the Order of St. John, the kingdom of Jerusalem, the Order of the Holy Sepulchre and the St. John's badge, with the word 'Jesus' in Aramaic script on the central tile. Three sets of these tiles are preserved in the collection at Clerkenwell[65] and Pirie-Gordon donated his to his local church in

Crickhowell in Wales, to be displayed above the effigy of medieval knight, Sir Grimbald de Pauncefote, who was said to have gone on crusade.[66] An account of the pilgrimage by Edwin King was published later the same year and the Maltese artist Edward Caruana Dingli depicted those present at the investiture at Malta in a large painting now in the church at Clerkenwell (Figure 3.2).

Not all the reporting was, however, positive and there were still those who challenged the legitimacy of the Order. The *Catholic News* described the pilgrimage as taking place under false colours:

> It is extremely irritating to those who know the facts to find the bogus English Order constantly referred to in the press as if it were not only the legitimate successor of, but absolutely identical with the ancient and illustrious Order, which of course still exists and is recognised as a Sovereign Order in Rome and in every catholic country in Europe.[67]

Centenary celebrations

In June 1931, the Order celebrated the centenary of its revival. The Sub Prior, the Earl of Scarborough noted:

> The purpose was to celebrate a Revival, not a creation, for that goes back to the eleventh century. It marks the centenary of a date when fresh life was breathed into the Order in England, which had lain dormant since the days of Queen Elizabeth. Looking back over the period since this Revival, the important point to note is that the prevailing desire of its pioneers was to seek inspiration from the very origin of the Order's creation, to those earliest days in Jerusalem when the spirit of service for the sick and suffering was the mainspring of its existence. Their aim was to infuse into our modern life that same spirit.

Members attended from across the world and there were receptions, royal investitures, banquets and parades. A congregation of 1,500 attended the centenary service in Westminster Abbey on 24 June, with a sermon preached by the Archbishop of Canterbury. The events were recorded in a centenary booklet published by the Order.[68]

The Order's work of course continues today with its history celebrated in the Museum at St. John's Gate and the Grand Prior is still a member of the royal family, the Duke of Gloucester.

Inspiring others

The Order inspired some other organisations. The Primrose League, founded in 1883 and dedicated to promoting a conservative ideology, took some of its practices from the Order of St. John, with members being given chivalric ranks (knights and dames) and the President described as Grand Master.[69]

And, as already mentioned, in the early 1900s, Harry Pirie-Gordon founded the Order of Sanctissima Sophia with the aim of reviving:

> The virtues of that period of the world's history commonly called the Middle Ages and to practice them, in the hope that we may thereby the better pursue wisdom as comprised in the Human Letters and Arts.

The details of its ceremonies, regalia and rules have clear echoes of the Order of St. John, of which Harry and his parents were proud members.[70]

The First World War led to the creation of some other chivalric orders, such as Olive Catherine Parr's White Knights and Ladies and the Knights of the Crucifix[71] and Mike Horswell has written about the short-lived Most Noble Order of Crusaders, established in 1921, which aimed to do works of charity for society and was led by a Grand Master.

Templars

The story of the Templars' trial and the dissolution of the Order is well chronicled and the various accounts published in Britain in the nineteenth century have been discussed in Chapter 1. The Order's British possessions were confiscated and most were transferred to the Order of St. John, but the story did not end there.

The legacy and developing myth of the Templars is both complicated and controversial. Claims of links between the Templars and freemasons first emerged in the eighteenth century and an unbroken list of Grand Masters from Jacques de Molay onwards was constructed.[72] One historian has commented:

> For conspiracy theorists, writers of pseudo history and many of their readers, the dramatic events of the early fourteenth century were simply a beginning of a new era in Templar history.[73]

The Templars also proved an inspiration for writers and their 'literary' legacy will be discussed in the next chapter.

This chapter will simply focus on two British aspects of this 'afterlife'; the attempt to revive the Templars in Britain in the 1820s and the Masonic Templars in Britain. It will look at some of those involved and the way in which they sought to link past and present.

Revival

Sir Sidney Smith, the hero of the 1799 siege of Acre, was a freemason, involved with both the neo-Templar Order in France and its short-lived British

Figure 3.3 Sir Sidney Smith wearing his Templar Cross, by Louis-Marie Autissier. Royal Collection Trust/© His Majesty King Charles III 2023.

counterpart.[74] He proudly wore a Templar cross, previously said to have been owned by Richard the Lionheart, which had been given to him by the Arch-bishop of Cyprus, in recognition of his having saved the islanders from insur-gents in 1799. He also claimed that the Archbishop had ordained him a Knight Templar and to have succeeded Grand Master Fabre de Palaprat as Regent in 1808. In his will, he left the cross to be worn by Grand Masters in perpetuity and he was depicted wearing it in various images such as a miniature by the French artist Louis-Marie Autissier.[75] Sir Harry Luke, himself a prominent member of the Order of St. John and Lieutenant Governor of Malta between 1930 and 1938, however, suggested that Smith's cross was probably made in the eighteenth century.[76] It is recorded as in the possession of the Order of St. John in Paris, but by the early twentieth century, it had reached the Royal Col-lection in London (Figure 3.3).[77]

Information about the revived Order in Britain is both patchy and unreli-able, but Richard Woof, already mentioned in connection with the Order of St. John, was an enthusiastic historian and his papers, in the collection of the Worcestershire Masonic Museum and Library,[78] shed some new light on the subject. As already noted, in 1865 he had published a *Sketch of the Knights Templars and the Knights Hospitallers of St. John of Jerusalem with notes on the Masonic Templars*, based on a paper which he had given to an encampment of the Masonic Templars meeting in his home town of Worcester. In this, he listed the members of the Order 'from an authentic source' and described some of their activities. He also claimed to have been enlisted as a Templar himself by Smith.[79]

In 1824/5, Augustus, Duke of Sussex, was appointed Grand Prior of England and 'in so doing, stipulated that no Englishman should be admitted into the Order without his special sanction'. Charles Tennyson D'Eyncourt, uncle of the poet Alfred Tennyson, MP for Stamford and then Lambeth and a romantic medievalist, was Prior of the London convent.[80] There was also a convent in Liverpool, but as this 'was established without the Duke's sanction, he never acknowledged its members'.[81]

Membership

Woof named 35 members of the Metropolitan Convent of London, including several Dukes and Earls, a naval officer, MPs, the historian Charles Mills and John James Watts.[82] Mills's biographer wrote:

It is well known that the ancient Order of Knights Templars has never ceased to claim an existence in Europe, with a regular and generally an illustrious succession of French Grand Masters, from the era of its famous persecution, in the fourteenth century, to the present time. The historian of the crusades, and of the Order of the Temple, was appropriately considered by that society an eligible member of their body; and Mr Mills was accordingly elected.[83]

The Order, however, seems to have been short-lived. Woof stated that no chapter of the Order had been held since 1836 and in 1865, he could name just eight surviving members of the London convent and five from Liverpool[84] This situation is confirmed in a letter from John James Watts to Edmund Lechmere dated May 1872. He recalled that Tennyson D'Eyncourt had decided not to join the Order of St. John, preferring:

with the cooperation of the old Admiral Sir Sidney Smith to introduce into England the Order of Knights Templars, which he did about 1825-6 and a very pleasant confraternity it was as I can testify being now one of only six survivors of the 34 original numbers. The other Templars existing at this day are the Duke of Leinster, the Marquis of Dorset, Lord Miltown, Lord Henry Cholmondeley, Mr. Wilson and myself.[85]

In his *Sketch of the History of the Knights Templar*, dedicated to the Duke of Sussex, Grand Prior of England by 'his faithful and obedient servant and brother', another member, James Burnes, wrote of the small numbers and the difficulty of joining:

> We regret to say that the Order of the Temple, notwithstanding its undeniable claims to honourable distinction, has never enjoyed much consideration amongst our countrymen. Its exclusive character, together with the great expense and difficulty which attend admission into its ranks, no Englishman being legitimately eligible, unless formally recommended by the illustrious Grand Prior of England, has raised against it a host of enemies...there are not more than 40 subjects of Her Majesty who are Knights Templars[86]

Smith had had ambitions for the knights to be 'armed mediators and pacificators, supporters of lawful authority and charitable institutions, protectors of the weak, the helpless and the oppressed, particularly females, orphans and the aged'. He had also wanted to establish a convent in Malta, to help liberate slaves and put down piracy. None of these ambitions, however, were realised. Of the key individuals, Smith died in 1840 and the Duke of Sussex in 1849. Tennyson D'Eyncourt seems to have lost interest and resigned in 1849.[87]

Depictions of Knights Templar in books, paintings and engravings probably owed more to Walter Scott[88] than the revived Order, but one recorded member, Dorset Fellowes, from a distinguished military family, who later served as Deputy Chamberlain to George IV, was painted by the artist Samuel Drummond in the costume of a Knight Templar. The work was shown at the Royal Academy in London in 1826 to a mixed reception. The *Monthly Magazine* commented:

> We had taken it for a groom covered with a horse cloth. The man seems alarmed, as if it was flung at him in some frolic of his fellow grooms, and the robe fits him as if it had been made for a quadruped seventeen hands high.[89]

The artist Richard Parkes Bonington also painted a romanticised *Knight Templar* in armour supported by two pages, which was copied by engravers and sold as a print.[90]

Some of those eager to attend the Eglington tournament in 1839 offered to appear 'in our Knight Templar dresses'[91] and Templars (or Scott's Sir Brian de Bois Guilbert) regularly appeared in the list of costumes at fancy dress balls. In Breconshire in Wales, a member of a local ironmaster's family appeared 'classically correct' as a Templar at a ball at the Dan y Parc estate in 1832 and the Hon. James Wortley wore a Templar costume at Queen Victoria's grand fancy dress ball in 1842.[92] With his love of history and costume, Harry Pirie-Gordon was also said to have attended an Oxford ball dressed as a Templar, 'taking part in a special quadrille with a lot of courtly sword play', although he did not take up the suggestion of his friend and later fellow member of the Order of Sanctissima Sophia, Frederick Rolfe, Baron Corvo, to write a history of the Order.[93]

Continuity and the Masonic order

There have been various other organisations which have used the term Templar to describe their members and activities, some with a charitable purpose such as the 'Good Templars' and the temperance movement, and others forming part of the masonic movement. In his history, Woof sought to disentangle the history of the Masonic Templars in Britain:

> An Order called the Masonic Knights Templars, Hospitallers of St. John of Jerusalem, Palestine, Rhodes and Malta has existed in this country for an uncertain period. Members being freemasons of a certain degree, were received into it as of the combined Orders of the Temple and St. John and their distinguishing badge, with other regalia, was a white enamelled cross of eight points charged with a cross pattee of red enamel and surmounted by the grand master's Crown worn from a red and white ribbon.

He added that the Masonic Templars 'being of a secret description...probably kept few records', but quoted one source which stated that the Order was introduced to Britain in November 1779.[94] Woof argued that the actual date was earlier, since there was a record of an encampment, which would have required some organisation, on the Isle of Wight in 1780 and a subsequent meeting at Winchester. Others give dates of 1791 or 1778.[95]

Woof himself was initiated into the Worcester Lodge of Freemasons in 1857 and became its Master in 1861. He went on to hold senior roles in the Worcestershire Order and beyond. The archives of the Worcester Masonic Museum also include evidence of gatherings throughout Britain, in, for example London, York, Bristol and Bath, with documents drawing on imagery from Templar history.

Another member from Worcestershire, Foster Gough, was inspired to research the history of the Templars:

> It is about ten years since I joined the Order of Masonic Knights Templar at Dudley...I was particularly impressed with the sublimity and beauty of their ceremonial-an impression which time, improved by study and experience, has only served to strengthen and confirm...I have sought to render myself conversant with all the details of the present symbolical institution, as well as to avail myself of many opportunities of becoming acquainted with the history, principles and peculiar characteristics of the original orders.[96]

Gough sources included Woof's *Sketch* and Addison's *History* and to reinforce the historic continuity, there were articles about the history of the crusades and the Templars in the *Freemasons' Magazine and Masonic Mirror*.[97] The masonic Templars also seem to have inspired popular literature in the form of ballads such as *The Knight Templar's Dream*, published in Glasgow, dating from c 1844 and priced at one pence.[98]

Woof traced the line of Grand Masters from 1791. Rather like those involved with early attempts to revive the English langue of St. John, they are a colourful cast of characters. In addition to the Duke of Sussex, Sir Thomas Dunckerly claimed to be an illegitimate son of George II; Walter Rodwell Wright was a barrister, author and diplomat, who spent his final years in Malta and Colonel Charles Kemeys Kemeys Tynte claimed an ancestor who had distinguished himself on the Third Crusade.[99]

Woof did not, however, accept all claims of a direct lineage from medieval Templars to masons:

> Very many well informed persons entertain no doubt that a connection between the Masonic Order and the ancient Templars existed (and is illustrated in the present Encampments) though not in the sense of the former being entitled to be considered knights by succession from the early Order. These persons are perhaps nearest the truth, and it is probably in this view of the subject that we must search for an explanation of the problem rather than by an endeavour to prove that the Masonic Order is the representative of the warrior monks in their chivalric capacity.[100]

He added the hope that new information might be found to 'dissipate that mystery which has so long surrounded the Masonic Templars'. Whatever the rival claims to antiquity of descent, he emphasised the key underlying principle of the Orders, namely charity.

Past and present

Reference has already been made to ceremonies celebrating the capture of Jerusalem in 1917 and on 12 December 1918, members of the United Religious and Military Orders of the Temple and of St. John gathered at the Temple church in London for their own service of thanksgiving marking the end of the First World War and the 'deliverance of the Holy Land'. In his sermon, the Master of the Temple, Revd. Barnes, who had preached at a similar service in December 1917, noted:

> It is most fitting that you should meet for this service in the Temple church. Your name shows that you seek to retain and foster the great ideals which animated the Knights Templars and the Knights of the Hospital before corruption and decay brought ruin or stagnation... as you come you wish to gather together the great memories of the past and to use them for inspiration and guidance in the present.[101]

The service was attended by the Duke of Connaught, not only Grand Prior of the Order of St. John, but also Grand Master of the Order of Masonic Knights

Templar and some 500 members of that Order. A collection was taken for the hospital of the Order of St. John in Jerusalem.[102] Other comparisons were drawn between those fighting in the War and the medieval Templars and the squadron of the Royal Flying Corps based at Copmanthorpe in Yorkshire, an area with past Templar associations, was known as the Knights Templar.[103]

Scottish Knights Templar

The Scotsman Andrew Michael Ramsay is regarded as the author of the pseudo history linking the medieval Templars with freemasonry and all that evolved from this.[104] There were also the stories of Templars who had fled from persecution in France and found refuge in Scotland. Writing in the mid-nineteenth century, Woof referred to a Grand Priory of Scotland with eight members, including several members of the Burnes family and Robert Bigsby.[105] And Alexander Deuchar, a seal engraver from Edinburgh from a family with Jacobite sympathies, established an independent Order of Knights Templar. He remained its Grand Master until 1836, when he was removed and replaced by Admiral David Milne, who held this office until his death in 1844.[106]

Another perspective

Not all shared the enthusiasm of members of the Order. The entry for the Templars in the 1911 edition of the Encyclopaedia Britannica, written by Walter Alison Phillips, was rather scathing about the modern Order:

> A delightfully absurd attempt to assert the continuity of the modern order of Knights Templar, which still has a considerable organisation in the US, with the suppressed Order, is made by Jeremy L. Cross in the Templar's Chart (New York, 184); he actually gives a complete list of Grand Masters from Hugues de Payns to Sir Sidney Smith (1838) and asserts that the encampment of Baldwin, which was established at Bristol by the Templars who returned with Richard 1 from Palestine, still continues to hold its regular meetings and is believed to have preserved the ancient costumes and ceremonies of the Order.[107]

Conclusion

The history of attempts to revive or reinvent the Orders in nineteenth-century Britain includes a cast of colourful characters and false dawns. For the Order of St. John, hard work and proven value led to the establishment and recognition of the Order which continues its valuable work today. In parallel its Museum and buildings record and celebrate the history of the medieval Order.

The British Association of the Sovereign Order of Malta similarly navigated hostility at a time of strong anti-catholic feeling and remains active in a variety of medical and humanitarian fields, not only in Britain but also across the world. The revival of the Templar Order in Britain is more complex. In a strict historical sense, the revived British Order only had a short life, but the memory of the Templars is now interwoven with the freemasonry and claims of continuity with the medieval Order. The painstaking researches of Richard Woof, who was himself a freemason, member of the revived Templar Order and the Order of St. John, offer some facts and clarity about this history, but what has been described as Templarism remains a dynamic field.

Notes

1 Gregory O'Malley, *The Knights Hospitaller of the English Langue 1460–1565* (Oxford, 2005), pp. 88, 320–32.
2 See Knobler, 'The Tsar's Crusade. Invented Holy War Tradition in Russia (1780–1920)', in *Nationalising the Crusades* ed. Horswell (Abingdon, 2023), p. 46.
3 *Edinburgh Review*, 1805, p. 205.
4 Kett, Henry, *Emily*, 2nd edition, 3 vols, vol. 3 (London, 1809) pp. 58 and 98. See also above, p. 58.
5 See Bigsby, p. 16 and Siberry, 'John Taaffe', *MO* 8 (forthcoming).
6 Charles Mills, www.odnb.com, accessed 18 April 2023.
7 Michael Hodges, *Roll of Deceased British Members of the Order of Malta from the 19th Century to 2018* (2019); Henry J.A. Sire, *The Knights of Malta* (New Haven, 1996), pp. 176–89.
8 Society of Antiquaries, WAT/0/28-30, 34.
9 George Bowyer, www.odnb.com, accessed 18 April 2023; Dorothy A. Heffernan, *Sir George Bowyer QC MP Knight of Malta* (Abingdon, 1983).
10 See Michael Wheeler, *Catholic and Protestant in Nineteenth Century English Culture* (Cambridge, 2006).
11 *The Times*, 25 November 1858, p. 7.
12 *Saturday Review*, 24 October 1863, pp. 557–8.
13 Elize de Montagnac, *Histoire des Chevaliers Hospitaliers de Sant-Jean de Jerusalem* (Paris, 1863). For Porter, see above, pp. 14–15.
14 *Saturday Review*, 24 October 1863. Bowyer was also caricatured as a Knight of Malta by Spy in *Vanity Fair* magazine in 1879.
15 https://historicengland.org.uk/listing/the-list/list-entry/1066244, accessed 18 April 2023. The church was subsequently rebuilt at the hospital's new location in St. John's Wood and Bowyer's heart is buried at the high altar.
16 See Hodges, which includes extracts from the 1876 Assembly minutes, pp. 115–8.
17 Riley-Smith, 'The Order of St. John in England, 1827–58', *MO* 1, 121–41.
18 Richard Woof, *A Brief Narrative of Circumstances Attending the Revival and Progress of the English Langue of the Order of St. John of Jerusalem*, 1872, unpublished, but surviving in the archives of the Museum of St. John (MOSJ), p. 8.
19 See Siberry, 'Images and Perceptions', p. 205 and below, p. 97.
20 Riley-Smith, *Hospitallers. The History of the Order of St. John* (London, 1999), p. 143.
21 For the fate and text of Hillary's pamphlet, see Siberry, *New Crusaders*, pp. 76–81 and Appendix B.
22 Taaffe, 4, p. 234.

23   Bigsby, *Memoir*, pp. 125–7.
24   Woof, *Brief Narrative*, p. 34.
25   Riley-Smith, 'Order of St. John in England', pp. 121, 132–41.
26   *Dublin Review* 46 (1859) pp. 480, 492–4.
27   BASOM Archives. Bowyer, *Early Correspondence Volumes*, letters dated 28
     September; 9 October; 27 November 1858; 21 January and 29 November 1859. I
     am grateful for the help of BASOM's archivist John Robinson and permission to
     quote from these documents.
28   Bryans, "Notes on Malta', p. 204.
29   *Notes and Queries*, 2nd series 10 (1860), 411, 460.
30   *Notes and Queries*, 3rd series 3 (1863), 8, 39, 76, 201–4, 252–4, 270–3, 278,
     289–91, 309–11.
31   *Notes and Queries*, 3 (1863), 331–4, 411–13, 450–1; 4 (1863), 11–12, 30, 92–3,
     190–1, 212–4.
32   'The Sovereign Order of St. John of Jerusalem and the English Langue', *Gentle-
     man's Magazine* n.s. 3:1 (1867), pp. 620–3.
33   Bigsby, *Memoir of the Illustrious and Sovereign Order of St. John of Jerusalem*
     (Derby, 1869).
34   Woof, *Brief Narrative*, p. 40.
35   Woof, *Brief Narrative*, pp. 8–10. The letter from Porter is filed in the Museum's
     copy of Woof's book.
36   *Order of St. John of Jerusalem. A Brief Notice of Its Foundation and Constitution
     and Its Objects in England* (London, 1878), pp. 9–10, 13.
37   See Edwin King, *The Knights of St. John in the British Realm*, revd. Sir Harry Luke
     (London, 1967), p. 146 and Nigel Hankin, 'Acquiring Heritage', p. 47.
38   *Reminiscences in the Life of Surgeon Major George A. Hutton* (London, 1907)
     pp. 145, 181–3.
39   *Northampton Daily Chronicle and Evening Herald*, 15 October 1887. See also
     Siberry, *Tales*, pp. 19–20; 30–26.
40   Riley-Smith, *Hospitallers*, pp. 131–40.
41   MOSJ, LDOSJ 9118.
42   King, *The Order of St. John and the British Empire* (London, 1934).
43   Siberry, *New Crusaders*, p. 65.
44   *The Times*, 19 July 1888, p. 12.
45   *The Times*, 6 April 1893, p. 4.
46   BASOM Archives, *Minute Book, General Assembly*, 1888.
47   *Punch*, 20 February 1897, p. 93.
48   King, *Order of St., John*, pp. 149–2.
49   Sophia Murphy, *The Duchess of Devonshire's Ball* (London, 1984), pp. 126–7.
50   Ardern Holt, *Fancy Dresses Described or What to Wear at Fancy Dress Balls*
     (London, 1887), p. 247.
51   See Hankin, 'Acquiring Heritage' pp. 43–62.
52   Hankin, pp. 45–6.
53   *Handbook of the Hungarian Market and General Eastern Bazaar in London to Be
     Opened on 28 June 1886 by Princess Beatrice* (London, 1886).
54   Thomas W. Wood and Henry W. Fincham, *An Illustrated Guide to the Remains
     of the Ancient Priory and the Present Parish Church of St. John at Clerkenwell*
     (London, 1903), p. 14; *The Times*, 22 May 1901, p. 10.
55   *The Times*, 12 June 1902, p. 5.
56   For the correspondence in 1787/8, see *Gentleman's Magazine*, 57 (1787), p. 460;
     58 (1788), p. 501. The history of the monument is described by Philip Whittemore,
     'Sir William Weston, Last Prior of the Order of St. John of Jerusalem d.1540',

Transactions of the London and Middlesex Archaeological Society 65 (2014), 271–81. See also Whitworth Porter, pp. 588–91. The dentist and antiquary, Theodosius Purland, is also said to have taken a cast of Weston's face. See Till, p. 14.

57 Memorial window: crypt east window and memorial plaque, MOSJ.

58 'The Capture of Jerusalem', *First Aid and the St. John's Ambulance Gazette*, January 1918, p. 100.

59 *St. John's Ambulance Gazette*, February 1918, pp. 116–7 and *The Times*, 12 January 1918, p. 3.

60 https://issuu.com/museumifhteorderofstjohn>docs; Chapter General 1918 and Lewer and Dark, p. 138.

61 Edwin King, *The Pilgrimage of 1926. Being the Official Journal of the Order of St. John* (London, 1926), p. vii.

62 Ibid.

63 William M. Duckworth, 'Pilgrimage to the Holy Land, under Cross of St. John, New Crusade, from Clerkenwell to Jerusalem', *Daily News*, 8 March 1926. A scrapbook at Clerkenwell contains numerous other press cuttings about of the pilgrimage and photographs.

64 Siberry, 'Variations on a Theme. Harry Pirie-Gordon and the Order of Sanctissima Sophia' in *Piety and Pugnacity*, *MO* 7, 237–47.

65 ''Tiles of Jerusalem', LDOSJ 3537-3541/1 MOSJ.

66 SIberry, 'A Crickhowell Crusader: The Case of the Missing Hands', *Brycheiniog* 16 (2013), 101–9.

67 *Catholic News*, 6 March 1926.

68 *The Centenary of the Revival of the Order of St John in England 1931* (St. John's Gate, 1932).

69 Janet H. Robb, *The Primrose League 1883–1906* (New York, 1968), p. 49.

70 Siberry, 'Variations on a Theme', p. 240.

71 Horswell, *Rise and Fall*, pp. 118–9 and 519–82.

72 Malcolm Barber, *The New Knighthood: A History of the Order of the Temple* (Cambridge, 1994), pp. 314–34; Michael Haag, 'The Templars. History and Myth, pp. 238–83; Peter Partner, The *Murdered Magicians*, pp. 89–180; Helen Nicholson, *The Templars*, pp. 266–77.

73 John Walker, 'The Templars Are Everywhere: An Examination of the Myths behind Templar Survival After 1307', *The Debate on the Trial of the Templars 1307–14*, ed. Jochen Burgtorf, Paul Crawford and Helen Nicholson (London, 2016), pp. 347–57.

74 See Siberry, ''Victorian Perceptions', pp. 366–7; Partner, pp. 139–40, 146, 149.

75 Harry Luke, *History of Cyprus*, 4 vols, vol. 4 (Cambridge, 1952) 4, pp. 100–3. See also Siberry, *New Crusaders*, pp. 72–6.

76 www.rct.org.uk, accessed 18 April 2023.

77 Lord Russell of Liverpool, *Knight of the Sword. The Life and Letters of Admiral Sir Sidney Smith* (London, 1964), p. 204.

78 www.worcestermasonicmuseum.co.uk. I am grateful to the Museum for their help.

79 Woof, *A Sketch of the Knights Templars*, p. 26.

80 For Tennyson, see Charles Tennyson and Hope Dyson, *The Tennysons. Background to Genius* (London, 1974), pp. 185–7; Mark Girouard, *The Return to Camelot* (Yale, 1981), pp. 69–76 and Siberry, 'Victorian Perceptions', p. 367.

81 Woof, p. 28.

82 Ibid., pp. 29–31.

83 Augustin Skottowe, *A Memoir of the Life and Writings of Charles Mills* (London, 1828), p. 71.

84 Woof, p. 28.

85   Letter to Edmund Lechmere from John James Watts 1872, MOSJ.
86   James Burnes, *A Sketch of the History of the Knights Templars* (Edinburgh, 1837), pp. 51–3.
87   Siberry,'Victorian Perceptions', pp. 367–8.
88   Scott gave a detailed description of Templar dress in *Ivanhoe*, see below, pp. 88–9.
89   *Monthly Magazine* (1826), p. 638.
90   See www.britishmuseum.org, accessed 11 August 2023.
91   Ian Anstruther, *The Knight and the Umbrella. An Account of the Eglington Tournament 1839* (Sutton, 1985), p. 168.
92   *Monmouthshire Merlin*, 12 November 1832; Coke Smyth album, www.vam.ac.uk, accessed 18 April, 2023.
93   Compton Mackenzie, *My Life and Times*, vol. 4 (London, 1965), p. 193 and Frederick Rolfe, *Letters to CHC Pirie-Gordon*, ed. Cecil Woolf (London, 1959), p. 43.
94   Woof, pp. 52–4.
95   See Partner, pp. 116, 189–24.
96   Foster Gough, *Narrative of the Knights Templar and Crusaders-Containing a Concise History of the Rise, Glory and Decline of the Grand Religious and Military Order of the Temple, with Some Account of the Knights Hospitaller Embracing the Causes and Results of the Crusades* (London, 1867), Preface.
97   See for example Anthony O'Neal Haye, 'The Knights Templars', *Freemasons' Magazine and Masonic Mirror*, 475 (6 August 1868), 101–4; 106–8.
98   *The Knight Templar's Dream*, Broadside Ballads (Glasgow, c. 1844). Another ballad, *Sons of Levi*, from c. 1840, described the initiation of a freemason recalling the past history of the Templars and Hospitallers. See also https://digital.nls.uk/broadsides/view, accessed 3 August 2023.
99   *Freemasons Monthly Magazine*, 1 December 1860, p. 18.
100   Woof, pp. 71–2.
101   Revd. E. Barnes, *The Deliverance of the Holy Land. A Sermon 1918*.
102   *The Times*, 13 December 1918, p. 11.
103   Trevor Wright, *"Knights Templar" The Copmanthorpe Squadrons of the Royal Flying Corps 1916–1918* (1991). See also, Horswell, pp. 118, 121 and 123.
104   See Barber, *New Knighthood*, p. 317.
105   Woof, pp. 31–2.
106   Robert Ferguson, *The Knights Templar in Scotland* (Stroud, 2013), pp. 149–51.
107   Encyclopaedia Britannica, *Templars*, 11th edition, vol. 26 (Cambridge, 1911), pp. 591–600.

4   Literary knights

The way in which the Knights of St. John and Knights Templar were portrayed in novels, poems, plays and opera, and related visual representations, was another factor in shaping the British memory of the Military Orders. The most famous, and perhaps infamous, depiction of a knight was probably the Templar Sir Brian de Bois Guilbert in Walter Scott's novel *Ivanhoe*. As will be discussed in this chapter, Sir Brian played to the negative view of the Templars, but even in the same novel, the perspective was more varied. Writers and composers were also inspired by events such as trial of the Templars and the death of the last Grand Master Jacques de Molay; the sieges of Rhodes in 1480 and 1522 and Malta in 1565. The literary quality of these works varied considerably, from major authors such as Scott and Robert Browning to the amateur poet printing a work for private circulation to friends and even pantomime, but, even if the substance of the poem, play or novel has not stood the test of time or would have been known to very few, such works shed light on the memory of the Orders through the author's use of sources and the way in which they display knowledge of and interest in Templar and Hospitaller history. Works published in France and Germany were also available both in their original language and translation and indirectly through journal reviews. The examples discussed below reflect the variety of this literary output.

Sir Walter Scott

The popularity of Scott's novels, running to numerous editions and translated into many languages meant that he dominated the image of the crusades and the Military Orders for many in the first half of the nineteenth century and remained influential for much longer. Indeed, what might be termed the Scott industry has left a lasting footprint and not just in Britain, with numerous editions, derivative works and translations.

Scott's interest in the Knights of St. John and visit to Malta will be discussed later in this chapter, but the Templars appeared in both *Ivanhoe* and *The Talisman*, the former published in 1819 and the latter in 1825, and both set against the background of the Third Crusade. In the *Talisman*, the crimes

DOI: 10.4324/9781003177234-5

and duplicity of the Grand Master are punished when he is executed by Saladin after the defeat at Hattin.[1] The Templar characters in *Ivanhoe* are more developed, from the cruel and proud Bois-Guilbert to the visiting Grand Master, Lucas de Beaumanoir and for this Scott drew on a range of sources, including a seventeenth-century translation of the Templar Rule.[2] *Ivanhoe* sold 10,000 copies in less than two weeks and was widely reviewed in the periodicals of the day. Editions were also illustrated by some of the leading contemporary artists and versions of the novel were produced for all ages and tastes, including the readers of gothic tales printed in the so-called Penny Dreadfuls.[3] An example of the latter was *The Crusader or the Witch of Finchley*, published as a free supplement to the *Work Girls of London* in 1865 as a cautionary melodrama, with the wicked baron Sir Brian de Bracy, who, like Bois Guilbert, abducts the Jewess Rachael (Rebecca).[4]

The reviews reflected a variety of views and often commented on the character of the Templars and by extension the Order itself. For example, *Blackwood's Magazine* wrote of Beaumanoir:

> A character drawn with great truth and skill, and admirably contrasted with those among whom he is called to mingle-grave, severe, bigoted, proud-but sincere, earnest, devout, adhering in word and deed to the old ascetic observance of the Temple, with a firm and sorrowful constancy, which produces a very pathetic effect.

The *Dublin Review*, however, accused Scott of an anti-catholic bias:

> It is rarely he paints his villains wholy bad, but he approaches this very nearly in his portraiture of the unfortunate but brave knights of the Temple...Scott places the Templars outside the pale of Christianity and chivalry, it therefore becomes imperative, while not disguising their faults, to show that they were not outside either as a body.[5]

Dramatisations and music

The story of *Ivanhoe* was very quickly picked up and adapted for various theatre audiences leaving a visual image of the characters before readers even had access to illustrated editions of the novel itself. At one point in 1820, there were five different stage adaptations playing in London, some including music and audiences in other towns throughout Britain such as Edinburgh, Birmingham, Worcester, Bury, Derby and Salisbury could also see versions of the novel. And it was not just performed by professional companies. For example, in 1854, the Pianoforte Makers Amateur Dramatic Benevolent Society produced the '*Romantic Drama*' *of Ivanhoe or the Knight Templar* at the Theatre Royal in London.

The extent of special effects which could be employed depended on the theatre, but *Ivanhoe* also appealed to producers of hippodrama, featuring, as the name implies, horses in a circus ring on stage and a key venue for this was Astley's amphitheatre in London, where *The Lists of Ashby or the Conquests of Ivanhoe* was performed in 1837.[6] In the decades following the novel's publication, the style of performance, and consequently depiction of the Templar, was increasingly tailored to specific audiences. Thus, the Christmas pantomime *Robin Hood and his merry men or Harlequin Ivanhoe, the Knight Templar and the Jewess*, by Colin Hazlewood, who was known for his farces and burlesques, staged at the Pavilion theatre in Whitechapel Road in London in 1867, combined comedy and fantasy. The stage directions include a wet Sir Brian appearing 'with umbrella up' and threatening Ivanhoe:

> Beware, for I feel as if a breath of mine, nay even a sneeze, or a blow on the nose, would give you a shiver de freeze.

Other characters include fairies of the woodlands and clowns and Isaac and Rebecca are saved by a Fairy Queen.[7]

As the villain, Bois Guilbert also found himself popularised in a variety of forms, from toy theatre to tinsel prints of actors playing the role.[8] His character was also drawn upon in political debate. In 1876, the poet Algernon Swinburne took up his pen to caricature the radical Birmingham MP, John Bright, who had defended the Bulgarian Christians against the Turks, in his *Ballad of Bulgarie*, as Sir Brian de Bromwicham, Knight Templar.[9]

Ivanhoe similarly inspired composers, including an opera by Rossini, which Scott himself saw in Paris in 1826 and was later performed in an English version at Covent Garden in 1829. Templar marches and songs were published for performance at home and Sir Julius Benedict's *March of the* Templars was played in 1887 as Queen Victoria entered Westminster Abbey for her golden jubilee service. Paintings of characters and scenes from *Ivanhoe* were also exhibited at, for example, the Royal Academy in London and characters from the novels were also chosen for costumes at fancy dress balls.[10]

Trial of the Templars and death of De Molay

The dramatic final days of the Order of the Temple and its members inspired other writers and readers in Britain and elsewhere.

The poet Robert Browning wrote a play, *The Return of the Druses*, featuring the Knights of St. John at Rhodes[11] and, interested in what he regarded as perversions of religion, in 1853–5, at a time of growing anti-catholic sentiment in Britain, he also penned a dramatic poem entitled *The Heretic's Tragedy* about the burning of de Molay, on 18 March 1314.[12] It took the form of a fictional theatrical performance some 200 years after the event, supposedly performed as part of the Roman Catholic festivals in Ypres. Some fellow writers such as Swinburne and G.K. Chesterton admired the work, but it does not seem to have been popular. Nevertheless, it shows again the way in which the history of the Templars was drawn upon by writers in response to contemporary events and concerns.[13]

The Templar story also inspired 'amateur' poets such as Thomas Billington. His 'poem with historical notes', *The Last of the Knights Templars*, privately published in 1886, surveyed the Order from its inception to the death of de Molay and the growing Ottoman threat. Billington explained that, confined to his bed with an illness, which, in fact, caused his death shortly before the poem appeared in print, he had rummaged 'among the lucubrations of former years, whence has been drawn out the Templar' and he seems to have been motivated by a desire to remind more critical contemporaries of the context in which the Orders had worked:

> Much acrimonious matter has, from time to time, been foisted in the public by writers attempting to prove the inutility, not to say disastrous consequences, attendant on the creation of the several military orders of knights, who once acted so prominent a part in the history of the old world. But if we consider the several ages in which they lived...we shall be less surprised that individuals should be found ready to unite themselves in a kind of brotherhood to answer the several ends in view.[14]

Billington's notes also shed light on his reading and access to works about the Order.

Ghostly Templars

As discussed in more detail in Chapter 2, the surviving material remains of the Templars also inspired some writers and their aged or ghostly Templars could be both good and evil. The novelist Charlotte Yonge, who wrote both stories and history books for children, described a visit to the ruined old refectory of the knights by her heroine Eustacie:

> to climb those winding stairs, and resign herself to be left alone with the Templars for the night, was by far the severest trial that had yet befallen the poor young fugitive...her memory reverted to the many tales of the sounds heard by night within those walls, church chants turning into diabolical sings and bewildered travellers into thickets and morasses, where they had been found in the morning, shuddering as they told of a huge white monk, with clanking weapons, and a burning cross of fire printed on his shoulder and breast, who stood on the walls and hurled a shrieking babe into the abyss.[15]

The notable writer of ghost stories, Montague James also had a destructive knight in his story *O Whistle, and I'll come to you, my lad*, but Rider Haggard, author of adventure stories, including one, *The Brethren*, set against the background of the Third Crusade, offered a more positive image of a former Templar in *Red Eve*. His white haired Father Arnold, veteran of campaigns in the East, now lives peacefully in the old preceptory of the Knights at Dunwich in Suffolk, with tattered banners and shields of past masters carved on the walls.[16]

The selection box of Templar history was also drawn upon by the playwright Angiolo Robson Slous, in his five act play entitled simply *The Templar*, which was performed at the Princess theatre in London in November 1850. Slous combined a story of a Templar who had joined the Order after fighting against the Cathars, with a love story between the daughter of one of his victims and the Grand Master's son and their reconciliation took place as King Philip IV of France announced the abolition of the Order.[17]

It starred two of the most successful actors of the day, Charles Kean and his wife Ellen and received generally favourable reviews. The *Athenaeum* reported, having read the play's text:

> The fable is romantic- made up of such well known ingredients as old revenge passion intercepted in its course by the Templar's vow. In arranging his material for the stage, Mr. Slous seems to have had reference to the powers of Mr. and Mrs. Charles Kean-to the former of whom the drama is inscribed. There is nothing here to shock in its monstrosity; nothing to divert by its bathos, though, on the other hand, there is little by novelty of situation, force of passion, or felicity of diction would justify quotation, we yet closed 'The Templar' inclined to believe that with pains and patience Mr. Slous may yet produce an acting play of fair merit.[18]

Another review, underlining the importance of the visual image in creating memory, as well as the words spoken, praised the costumes and scenery:

> The harmonies and contrasts of colour in the costumes, and the art with which the groupings are placed, are so complete, and have so settled a look of foregone studies, that we feel almost certain they must have been first sketched and coloured as pictures and the stage was then arranged in accordance with them.[19]

In short, something for everyone and a further illustration of how the Templars proved a fertile source for the British literary imagination.

Drama in translation

In 1805, the French writer Francois Raynouard's 5 act play, *Les Templiers* was performed in Paris, where it attracted the interest of Napoleon.[20] While there is no evidence that it was ever performed in Britain, it was reviewed by, for example, the *Edinburgh Review* in 1807. As discussed elsewhere in this book, such reviews show that contemporaries not only had access to information about literary works published outside Britain, but also expectations about their readers' knowledge of the subject and links were explicitly drawn with contemporary events. In this instance, the reviewer began by explaining that he would deal first with Raynouard's treatment of truth and then consider how he had succeeded with fiction. On the former, he noted that the subject for the tragedy was generally known to 'every person of education' and he was not impressed:

> When therefore we opened the volume before us and found that the tragedy was preceded by the history of the Templars, well garnished with too many citations, proofs and documents, we could not help thinking the conduct of the author injudicious.

He also considered the abridged history of the Order more 'rhetorical pleading' than 'a historical statement'. Writing against the background of the war with France, it does not seem to have been difficult to obtain a copy of the play for review:

> When we were first informed that the tragedy of the Templars had been represented with considerable success at Paris, we became anxious to obtain a copy of it. Within a few days of the time when we are now writing, this publication was put into our hands. The task of reviewing it has been greater than we reckoned for, as we did not expect to get a history into the bargain. It has, however, afforded us some consolation to think that we may perhaps be enabled to amuse our readers by giving them an account of a drama which has pleased at Paris. They will make their own reflections on the very different tastes for theatrical exhibitions which prevail in the two greatest capitals of Europe.

The reviewer thought that there were some 'fine passages and many excellent verses', but that, as a playwright, Raynouard was not the equal of his seventeenth-century predecessors Corneille or Racine. He concluded by quoting from the speech of King Philip IV after his defeat of King Edward III of England, adding 'we can applaud the lines and smile at the allusion'.[21]

Raynouard of course also published documents relating to the trial of the Templars in his *Monuments Historiques* from 1813 and reviewed again in the *Edinburgh Review* in 1900.[22]

Nathan der Weise

The Templars were portrayed differently in the German philosopher and dramatist Gotthold Ephraim Lessing's 1779 play *Nathan der Weise,* set in

Jerusalem against the background of the Third Crusade. This was never performed in Lessing's lifetime, but the subject of tolerance between Islam, Christianity and Judaism prompted a number of British writers and publishers to produce English translations of variable quality. They came from very different backgrounds and professions, suggesting that the play was quite widely known and attracted significant interest. The first English translation was produced by the exiled German scientist and librarian, Rudolph Erich Raspe, in 1781 and he was followed by William Taylor of Norwich in 1791, the Scottish surgeon Robert Willis in 1868 and Major General Patrick Maxwell in 1896. Reviews of Lessing's work could be found in periodicals such as the *Saturday, Westminster* and *Edinburgh Reviews*. In May 1860, the *Saturday Review* discussed a recently published translation by Dr. Adolphus Reich, which included a biography of the author and critical analysis of his work. The reviewer did not think much of Reich's skills as a translator, but the article provided a platform both for a summary of the history of the Templars and analysis of Lessing's advocacy of religious toleration. And in 1864, the same magazine commented on a critical analysis of the play by the German philosopher Kuno Fischer.[23] Advertisements for other editions and translations, including those for use in schools, in contemporary periodicals `are another indication of interest in the work.[24] Incidentally, Lessing's great nephew Karl was also attracted by the subject of the crusades, producing several paintings of a returning crusader.[25]

Zacharias Werner

The German romanticist and freemason Zacharias Werner wrote two dramatic poems featuring the Templars, known as *Die Sohne des Thais (The Sons of the Valley)* in 1803/4, but individually titled- *Die Templer auf Cypern* (The Templars in Cyprus) and *Die Kreuzesbruder* (The Brethren of the Cross). They were translated into English in 1886 and 1892 respectively, but known and available to British readers in German much earlier. They were also reviewed and discussed in some detail in Thomas Carlyle's essay on Werner published in 1839. Carlyle played an important part in bringing the works of German writers to a British audience and, while he criticised Werner's use of mystical theology and 'masonic mummery', he quoted extensively in English from the play and thereby brought it to wider attention.[26] Werner's interest in the crusades was also reflected in his use of crusade language to campaign against Napoleon[27] and he wrote a play about the Teutonic knights *Das Kreuz an der Ostsee* (The Eastern Crusade) (1806).

Die Templer takes place in Limasol, Cyprus in 1306, before the downfall of the Templars but when they 'are but shadows of their old renown'. It has a cast of characters from Molay to two mystical figures Edo and Australis and a Scottish knight Sir Robert of Heredon and is woven through with ideas of freemasonry and gnosticism. It ends with de Molay receiving a summons to go to France. *Die Kreuzbruder* is set eight years later in Paris in March 1314 and ends with the death of Molay. The titular Sons of the Valley are a Carmelite body, who intrigue against the Templars and the poems tell the story of a group of Templars who escape to Scotland and provide a link with later Freemasonry.

The English translator was Elizabeth Lewis and her family background and the choice of publisher provide further insights into interest in the subject. Lewis was the granddaughter of the Earl of Carnarvon and the wife of Algernon Herbert, a London lawyer. Her translator footnotes reveal her own reading, from Addison's history of the Order to Scott's *Ivanhoe*, and Carlyle. She also refers to a *History of France* by the popular historian Mrs. Markham, and Samuel Beeton's *Encyclopaedia of Universal History*. And for the charges levelled at the Templars, she quotes the analysis published by the lawyer John Morshead, who wrote as J. Shallow.[28] This eclectic mix was probably typical of the pot pourri of sources on which those interested in the subject of the Templars could draw and which shaped their knowledge of the Order. Lewis noted in her Preface to the second volume that her interest in the poem began with a friend who did not know German, but 'raised a free lance against Gnosticism in any form'. She would have been aware of claims of Templar continuity and expressed her own firm views:

> If, however, it be a fact that the Templars carried to the remote Hebrides their dead Phoenix there to resuscitate in silence and mystery its ashes, the act cannot be proved historically or in the ordinary way of literature. It rests with the Freemasons body to verify it out of their private archives which are inaccessible to the uninitiated, and this maybe they cannot do, and probably would not if they could. In default of this verification, it is a good deal to be asked to believe that the mysteries slumbered in Scotland from 1314 to 1688 when freemasonry first manifested itself in the political interests of the Stuarts.[29]

Lewis's translation of Werner's poems would certainly have brought the issue to a wider readership. *The Templars* appeared in Bohn's popular Standard Library series and *The Brethren* was published by the owner of Bohn, George Bell.

Opera

Operas inspired by Scott, as already noted, offered ample opportunity to portray Templar knights and Jules Massenet, Pascal Prosper and Henry Charles Litolff all composed operas entitled *Les Templiers*, in 1873, 1867 and 1886 respectively. They were, however, never performed in London and seem to have attracted only brief attention across the English channel.[30]

Knights of St. John

Siege of Rhodes. 1480 and 1522–3

The Ottoman Turks besieged Rhodes in 1480, when they were repelled and again in 1522–3, when they captured the island and forced the knights to seek refuge elsewhere. Reference has already been made to histories of the knights' occupation and defence of Rhodes and these had some literary echoes.

The 1480 defence of Rhodes had inspired a romantic tale or novel-*Heloise or the Siege of Rhodes*-by George Monck Berkeley published in 1788 and the 1522 siege of Rhodes was the subject of an opera by William Davenant in 1656; the year of the Venetian defeat of Ottoman naval forces at the Dardanelles.[31] In the nineteenth century, it inspired some writers such as Sir James Bland Burges, who had also written an epic poem about Richard the Lionheart.[32] In 1805, he produced a play *The knight of Rhodes*, a tragic love story set against the background of the siege.[33] The popular novelist G.P.R. James, also published a novel *Bertrand de la Croix* in 1831, making his hero the nephew of the Grand Master. And Walter Scott was said to have considered writing a poem on Rhodes and had a collection of notes on the subject in his library, provided by his friend Sir William Gell.[34]

The first siege also inspired the prolific writer of historical adventure stories for children, George Henty. In 1895/6, he published *A Knight of the White Cross* and introduced his subject as follows:

> The Order was the great bulwark of Christendom against the invasion of the Turks and the tale of their long struggle is one of absorbing interest, and of the many eventful episodes none is more full of incident and excitement that the first siege of Rhodes.[35]

Henty was not uncritical of the knights who 'passed their slothful ease at their commanderies', but his hero and exemplar for his young readers was the English knight Sir Gervaise Tresham, who sent a force commanded by his eldest son to defend the island again in 1522 and provided financial support to the knights when they moved to Malta.

More research is still needed on the way in which the subject of the crusades and the Military Orders was taught in schools (of all descriptions), but Henty was clear that the objective of his books was to teach history and Mike Horswell has written about his influence in 'creating chivalrous imperial crusaders'. Young and indeed older readers would have consumed a rich diet of works (fact and fiction), which used the example of the past to inspire them to fight for the British empire and do their chivalrous duty.[36]

Siege of Malta

The knights' heroic defence of their island against the Ottoman Turks inspired a dramatic 'tragedy' intended 'to recommend as objects of imitation the pure and the virtuous of character' published in 1823.[37] And in 1829, the actress turned author, Ann Catherine Holbrook, turned her hand to an historical tale entitled *Constantine Castriot*, the Greek Prince who was involved in the siege. Holbrook explained her choice of subject as follows:

> A few years ago, I accidentally met with an account of the attack upon the Knights of Malta by Solyman…struck with the heroism the Christians displayed during the contest, I felt irresistibly inclined to throw the acts in paper, and to the dry detail of the historian, add the enlivening aid of probable embellishment. A pious interest is naturally excited in the perusal, as we contemplate to what pitch valour combined with moral zeal can elevate the human character.[38]

This was another moral tale and it is not clear whether either work attracted much interest or readership, but *The Knight of St. John: A Romance*, published in 1816 by the popular novelist Anna Maria Porter, would certainly have been more widely read. It told the story of the young knight of St. John, Giovanni Cigala, and made frequent reference to the noble history of the Order and the duty 'of every Christian, but especially of every knight, to rally round the standard of St. John'. Appearing in the popular three volume format favoured by circulating libraries such as Mudies in London, it was said to have been the last book read aloud to Princess Charlotte, daughter of King George IV, by her husband Prince Leopold the day before she died.[39]

Scott and Malta

Walter Scott approached the subject in a different way. His collection of arms and armour included a helmet which had 'belonged to a warrior who had fought in the Holy Land as there is a red Maltese cross engraved on it'[40] and in the autumn of 1831 he travelled to Malta with his copy of Vertot in hand. He had already been thinking about a work about the Knights of St. John for the fourth series of *Tales of a Grandfather*, but once in Malta he began to write what became another historical novel, *The Siege of Malta*. Staying with his friend John Hookham Frere, Scott visited the sites associated with the knights and the church of St. John in Valletta and Frere presented him with a set of prints of the siege which he took back to his library at Abbotsford, where they remain.[41]

Scott's *Siege* did not find favour with his publishers and was not published in his lifetime. In 1942, it formed the basis of a novel by Sydney Fowler Wright,[42] but in 2008 it finally appeared in a modern edition in the Edinburgh University

Press edition of Scott's novels.[43] Another writer of heroic tales for children, army medical officer, Lieut. Colonel Frederick Brereton, published *A Knight of St. John* subtitled *A Tale of the Siege of Malta* in 1906. In later years, his main characters meet on the anniversary of the 'relief of Malta' and recall 'when each held his post in the breach and fought proudly for the Order as a Knight of St. John'.[44]

Newdigate prize 1836 and other poems

As already noted, the choice of the Knights of St. John as the subject for the annual poetry competition at Oxford in 1836 is intriguing and may reflect the interest in the revival of the English langue during this period. The winner of the competition was Frederick Faber, who was later known as a theologian and hymn writer and converted to Roman Catholicism in 1847. His poem charted the Order's history from 'Acre's ramparts' to Rhodes, the 1565 siege of Malta and British rule:

> England's pennon now
> Floats gaily o'er St. Elmo's castled brow,
> Beneath that guardian pennon, undismayed
> Wealth's busy votaries ply their peaceful trade…while the white city,
> strong in faith and love…
> Wraps old memories round her, like a spell.[45]

Henry Burrows, later a Canon of Rochester cathedral among other ecclesiastical preferments, also entered a poem for the competition, which was subsequently published privately. He had been born in Malta in 1816, the son of an army officer based there, so the subject had a natural attraction.[46]

Another writer inspired by the knights styled himself IROG and took the story up to the loss of Malta in 1798 and Frank Fellows, a member of the Order, produced a curious work which moves between history and dreams of love. Privately printed in 1890, it was dedicated to the Princess of Wales, a Dame Chevalier of the Order, and told of knights:

> Who held ever high the white eight pointed cross, who by noble thoughts and deeds nourished a lustre bright upon the history of the most famous knightly order old.[47]

A Knight of St. John also featured in a posthumously published novel, *Gaston de Blondeville* by Mrs. Radcliffe, better known for gothic novel *The Mysteries of Udolpho*. Set in the reign of King Henry III, Gaston is accused of the murder of his kinsman, Reginald de Folville, a Knight of St. John returning from crusade. The knight's murder in the forest of Arden is re-enacted in a pageant held at Kenilworth castle before the king with the true culprit identified and the knight's burial place duly located in the Abbey of St. Mary's.[48] Another tale of right triumphing over evil.

Conclusion

The fictionalised story of the Military Orders and their knights was therefore available in a variety of publications and forms. Scott, and in particular, his Templar Sir Brian de Bois Guilbert, was undoubtedly the primary source for many, because of his popularity and the way in which his novels were reproduced from print to paintings, plays, operas and popular editions for wider consumption and readers and audiences of all ages and tastes. As discussed above, however, the subject inspired a variety of other writers, both well-known and long forgotten and literary forms, including the gothic novel and pantomime. The great sieges of Rhodes and Malta also provided a platform for tales of heroic deeds by young knights providing an example to follow in more modern times. In addition, British readers had access to works published elsewhere, either in the original French or German or translation and, if they did not read the original, they would have been aware of the subject matter from periodical reviews and advertisements. The Templars and Knights of St. John were therefore familiar literary figures and this would have contributed to the tapestry of memory and knowledge of their history.

Notes

1 See Barber, *The New Knighthood*, pp. 328–31.
2 See above, pp. 22.
3 Scott, *Ivanhoe; Introduction and Notes from the Magnum Opus. Ivanhoe to Castle Dangerous* eds. J.H. Alexander, Peter Garside and Claire Lamont (Edinburgh, 2012), pp. 1–4. For the gothicisation of *Ivanhoe*, see James Rymer, *The Black Monk* (1844) and Siberry, *Tales*, p. 97.
4 See Siberry, *New Crusaders*, p. 157.
5 *Blackwoods Magazine* 6 (1819/20), p. 267; Thomas Canning, 'Catholicism in the Waverley Novels', *Dublin Review* 26 (1891), 340–1.
6 For the variety of dramatisations, see Barbara Bell, "…anything like the words": How Stage Performances from *Ivanhoe* Brought Scott's Characters to the Widest Audiences', *The Wensham Review of Literature and Culture* 13 (2) (2020), 69–97 and Philip Cox, *Novels and Verse Narratives on the Stage 1790–1840* (Manchester, 2000), pp. 77–120.
7 Colin H. Hazlewood, *Words and Songs of the Christmas Pantomine (sic) Entitled Robin Hood and His Merry Men* (London, 1867).
8 For tinsel prints, see https://collections-vam.ac.uk/item/0158313/john-pthomas-haines-as-brian-tinsel-print, accessed 11 August 2023.
9 See Vesna Goldsworthy, *Inventing Ruritania. The Imperialism of the Imagination* (New York, 2013), pp. 41–5 and Timothy A.J. Burnett, 'Swinburne's "The Ballad of Bulgarie"', *Modern Language Review* 64 (1969), 276–82.
10 See Siberry, *New Crusaders*, pp. 122–29 and 'Victorian Perceptions', p. 371.

11 Robert Browning, 'The Return of the Druses: A Tragedy', *Poetical Works*, ed. Ian Jack, 15 vols, vol. 3 (Oxford, 1983–2009), pp. 441–9. It was never performed and much criticised by his friend the actor William Macready in August 1840. See *Elizabeth Barrett Browning and Robert Browning. Interviews and Recollections*, ed. Martin Garrett (Basingstoke, 2000), pp. 44–5.

12 Robert Browning, 'The Heretic's Tragedy', *Poetical Works*, vol. 5, pp. 441–9.

13 John H. Baker, 'The Influence of Robert Southey's "the Origin of the Rose" on Robert Browning's "The Heretic's Tragedy"'. *Westminster Research: Papers in Literary Studies*, https://westminsterresearch.westminster.ac.uk/papers-in-literary-studies, accessed 14 April 2023.

14 Thomas Billington, *The Last of the Knights Templar* (Preston, 1866), pp. 57–8.

15 Charlotte Yonge, *The Chaplet of Pearls* (London, 1868). Chapter 17 is entitled The Ghosts of the Templars.

16 Rider Haggard, *Red Eve* (London, 1911), pp. 30–33, 258–9. See also Siberry, *New Crusaders*, p. 156. For James, see Nicholson, *Templars*, pp. 270–5.

17 Angiolo Slous, *The Templar: a Play in Five Acts and Verse* (London, 1850).

18 *Athenaeum*, 28 September 1850, pp. 1015–6.

19 Tallis's Dramatic Magazine and General Theatrical and Musical Review (1850), p. 54.

20 Alain Demurger, 'The Knights Templar between Theatre and History: Raynouard's Works on the Templars', (1805–13) *MO* 3, 45–52. See also Partner, pp. 137–8.

21 'Les Templiers, tragedie preceded d'un precis historique sur les templiers par M. Raynouard', *Edinburgh Review* 107 (1805), 196–211.

22 See above, p. 19.

23 *Saturday Review*, 26 May 1860, pp. 686–7 and 24 September 1864, pp. 400–1.

24 Sydney H. Kenwood, 'The Influence of Lessing in England', *Modern Language Review* 9 (1914), 344–58.

25 See Siberry, *New Crusaders*, p. 172.

26 Thomas Carlyle, *The Life and Writings of Werner'* in *Critical and Miscellaneous Essays* (London, 1869), pp. 103–68.

27 See Colin Walker, 'Zacharias Werner and the Crusade against Napoleon', *Bulletin of the John Rylands Library* 71 (3) (1989), 141–57 and Siberry, 'Crusading against France', forthcoming.

28 Zacharias Werner, *The Brethren of the Cross*, trans. Elizabeth Lewis (London, 1882) and *The Templars in Cyprus*, trans. Lewis (London, 1886). For Lewis's references to her sources, see, for example, in *Templars*, pp. 17, 133, 149, 194 (Addison); pp. 27, 28, 85, 101 (*Ivanhoe*); p. 174 (Carlyle); p. 130 (Markham); in *Brethren*, p. 61 (Beeton); pp. 13, 20 and 21 (Shallow).

29 *Brethren*, pp. vii–viii and 206.

30 Brief references can be found to Pascal and Litolff's operas in the *Athenaeum*, 13 July 1867, p. 59 and 21 March 1885, p. 386.

31 Judy H. Park, 'The Limits of Empire in Davenant's The Siege of Rhodes', *Mediterranean Studies* 24 (2016) 47–76. See also Maclellan, pp. 4–5.

32 See Siberry, 'Crusading against France', forthcoming.

33 Sir James Burges, 'Knight of Rhodes' in *Dramas* (London, 1817).

34 Edith Clay, 'Rhodes: Sir William Gell to Sir Walter Scott', *Journal of the Warburg and Courtauld Institute* 33 (1970), 336–43.

35 George Henty, *A Knight of the White Cross*, (London, 1895/6), Preface, pp. v–vi.

36 Horswell, *British Medievalism*, pp. 76–9.

37 Anon. *The Siege of Malta*. A tragedy in five acts and in verse (London, 1823).

38 Ann Holbrook, *Constantine Castriot; An Historical Tale* (London, 1829).

39 Anna Maria Porter, *The Knight of St. John* (London, 1817).

40 Scott, *Letters*, 5 vols. ed. H.J.C. Grierson (London, 1932–7), 5, p. 396.

41 Scott, *Siege of Malta and Bizarro*, pp. 405–11. See also Donald Sultana, *The Siege of Malta Rediscovered. An Account of Sir Walter Scott's Mediterranean Journey and Last Novel* (Edinburgh, 1977) and above, pp. 11.

42 Sydney Fowler Wright, *Siege of Malta, Founded on an Unfinished Romance by Sir Walter Scott* (London, 1972).

43 Scott, *Siege of Malta*, pp. 323–8.

44 Frederick Brereton, *A Knight of St. John* (London, 1906), p. 384.

45 Frederick Faber, 'Knights of St. John', *Poems* (London, 1856), p. 123. See also Siberry, *New Crusaders*, pp. 134–5.

46 Henry Burrows, *Knights of St. John* (Oxford, 1892).

47 IROG, The Knights of St. John of Jerusalem afterwards of Rhodes and Malta (London, 1838); Frank Fellows, in *Memoriam and Knights Hospitallers* (London, 1890).

48 Ann Radcliffe, *Gaston de Blondeville* (London, 1833).

5 Conclusion

As the above chapters have described, the way in which the Order of St. John and Templars were remembered in Britain in the late eighteenth, nineteenth and early twentieth centuries was derived from a variety of different sources and these still influence their reception today. Some are well known, but this study has drawn on a range of new material to be found in the archives of the Orders themselves and other national and regional collections, as well as using sources which have hitherto received little attention, such as periodical reviews, correspondence and articles. The first book-length survey of the subject, it has also identified avenues for future research and analysis, from the decisions made by publishers commissioning histories of the Orders to the way in which the subject was taught in schools and the interaction between the ambitions of the Order of St. John and British foreign policy in the Mediterranean.

The greater availability and diversity of published histories and original sources was a key component in informing and shaping the memory of the Orders and, in the case of the Order of St. John, interest would also have been stimulated by visits to Rhodes and Malta, with the latter becoming a British crown colony and important military base. The fate of the Templars also intrigued and inspired historians to analyse the source material and, in some instances, mount a defence against the charges levelled against them. Such works were not confined to library shelves; they were also analysed in the numerous periodicals of the day and thereby reached a much wider readership. References to reading about the Orders can also be found in contemporary letters and diaries.

In addition, the material remains of the Orders in Britain, not least the Temple church in London, intrigued local antiquarians and the legal successors of the Templars, who lived and worked in the Inner and Middle Temple and worshipped in the church consecrated by Patriarch Heraclius in 1185. Here they celebrated major events, not least the capture of Jerusalem in December 1917 and the sermons preached on these occasions and related newspaper accounts drew clear parallels between the past and present and shared traditions of service and sacrifice. St. John's Gate and church in Clerkenwell

DOI: 10.4324/9781003177234-6

also became the focus for the material memory of the revived Order of St. John in Britain. More generally, the restoration of sites linked with the Orders enabled their new owners to commission works commemorating the knights particularly in the medium of stained glass.

Emerging from the loss of their Maltese home in 1798, the Order of St. John began to lay new foundations. The catholic Sovereign Order found a new base in Rome and its British Association was finally established in 1875. In the interim, there were discussions about the revival of the English langue in largely Protestant Britain, with a cast of colourful characters. It proved to be a rollercoaster ride, but firm foundations were laid in the 1860s and 1870s, followed by royal recognition and the establishment of a hospital in Jerusalem and the St. John Ambulance Association. Celebrating and displaying its history was central to its work and headquarters at Clerkenwell.

The history of the Templars was, of course, very different. Efforts to revive the Order in Britain (the neo Templars) were short-lived, but the history of the Order was drawn on extensively by the masonic Templars and some individuals were simultaneously members of the Order of St. John, the neo Templars and the freemasons.

To add to the tapestry of memory, the Orders and particularly the Templars, inspired a variety of writers. Prominent among these was, of course, Sir Walter Scott and his literary footprint was immense, from editions of his novels to spin off dramas performed throughout Britain aimed at different audiences, operas, music and art. The character of the Templar, Sir Brian de Bois Guilbert, from Ivanhoe, captured the readers' imagination and he was depicted in various forms, from prints to penny dreadfuls. A variety of other writers, both well-known and long forgotten, were also inspired by the history of the Orders and the imprint made by the written word was supplemented by illustrations and engravings. There was in practice no rigid boundary between history and fiction and younger readers would have learnt about the Orders from novels and tales of adventure, inspiring them to noble deeds like the knights of old. The British reader would also have been aware of works published elsewhere in Europe and in other languages and their footnotes and bibliographies provide further evidence of wide reading.

The memory of the Military Orders was therefore based on and created by a rich mix of historical writing, material remains, literature and popular fiction and the revived or reinvented Orders drew heavily on their medieval past to underpin their work and justify their existence.

Bibliography

Primary

Manuscripts

BASOM Archives. George Bowyer Early Correspondence;
———. Minute book General Assembly, 1888;
Dorset Archives. Receipted bill for work in the church of Stock Gaylard. PE-SKG/
  CW/2/1 and AQ/1.0.
Harriet Edgeworth, Bodleian Library, Archives and manuscripts. MS Eng. Lett. 745,
  fol. 106–8.
Inner Temple, London Archives. BUI/9/2. Inner Temple Hall: Hall Building Committee
  Minutes. Enclosed correspondence and papers concerning the decoration, windows
  and bronze figures for the new Hall and rough minutes 1870–7.
Museum of the Order of St. John: https://issuu.com/museumoftheorderofstjohn/docs,
  Chapter General 1918;
———. Letter Edmund Lechmere to J. J. Watts 1873;
———. 'Tiles of Jerusalem', LDOSJ 3537–3541/1;
———. LDOSJ 9118;
John James Watts. WAT/0/28-30, 34. Society of Antiquaries.
Whyte family correspondence. MSS 19. Yale Center for British Art.

Printed material

Addison, Charles Greenstreet. *Damascus and Palmyra: A Journey to the East.* London:
  Bentley, 1838.
———. *The Temple Church.* London: Longman, 1843.
——— and Robert Macoy. *The Knights Templar and the Complete History of Masonic
  Knighthood from the Origins of the Orders to the Present Time.* New York: Masonic
  Publishing Company, 1873.
Anonymous. *The Siege of Malta: A Fragment of the History of the Sovereign Order of
  St. John.* Newcastle: G. B. Richardson, 1850.
Badger, George Percy. *Description of Malta and Gozo.* Malta: M. Weiss, 1838.
Barnes, Revd. E.W. Jerusalem. *A Sermon Preached in Commemoration of the Capture
  of Jerusalem.* London: Inner and Middle Temple, 1918.
———. *The Deliverance of the Holy Land. A Sermon.* London, 1918.
Baylis, Henry. *The Temple Church and Chapel of St. Ann.* London: Philip, 1893.

Bedford, William K.R. and Richard Holbeche. *The Order of the Hospital of St. John of Jerusalem Being a History of the English Hospitallers of St. John, Their Rise and Progress.* London: Robinson, 1902.

Bellot, Hugh H.L. *The Inner and Middle Temple. Legal, Literary and Historic Associations.* London: Methuen, 1902.

Bigsby, Robert. *Memoir of the Illustrious and Sovereign Order of St. John of Jerusalem.* Derby: Richard Keene, 1868.

Billings, Robert W. *Architectural Illustrations and Account of the Temple Church.* London: T. and W. Boone, 1838.

Billington, Thomas. *The Last of the Knights Templar.* Preston: Henry Thomson, 1866.

Boisgelin, Louis de. *Ancient and Modern Malta and Also the History of the Knights of St. John of Jerusalem.* 2 vols. London: G. and J. Robinson, 1804.

Brereton, Frederick. *A Knight of St. John.* London: Blackie, 1905.

Britton, John. *The Architecture and Antiquities of Britain.* 5 vols. London, 1807–26.

Browning, Elizabeth Barrett and Robert. *Interviews and Recollections,* ed. Martin Garrett. Ashgate: Basingstoke, 2000.

———. Robert. *Poetical Works.* 15 vols. ed. Ian Jack. Oxford: OUP, 1983–2009.

Bryans, James William. 'Notes in Malta and the Knights Hospitallers', *Colburn's United Service Magazine* 101 (1863), 191–205.

Brydone, Patrick. *A Tour through Sicily and Malta in a Series of Letters to William Beckford.* 1773.

Burges, Sir James. *Dramas.* London: J. Cawthorn, 1805.

Burnes, James. *A Sketch of the History of the Knights Templars.* Edinburgh: Blackwood, 1837.

Burrows, Henry. *Knights of St. John.* Oxford: privately printed, 1892.

Byron, Lord George. *Letters and Journals of Lord Byron with Notices of His Life*, ed. Thomas Moore. 2 vols. London: J. and J. Harper, 1830.

Caoursin, Guillaume de. *Account of the Siege of Rhodes*, ed. Henry W. Fincham. St. John's Gate, 1926.

Carlyle, Thomas. 'The Life and Writings of Werner' in *Critical and Miscellaneaous Essays.* 6 vols. London: Chapman and Hall, 1869.

Centenary of the Revival of the Order of St. John in England 1931. London: St. John's Gate, 1933.

Clark, Hugh. *Concise History of Knighthood, Containing the Religious and Military Orders Which Have Been Instituted in Europe.* London: W. Strahan, 1784.

Clarke, George T. 'The Babingtons, Knights of St. John', *Archaeological Journal* 36 (1878), 219–30.

Darling, Charles. *Inner Templars Who Volunteered and Served in the Great War.* London: Whittingham and Griggs, 1917.

Dobson, Susannah. *Historical Anecdotes of Heraldry and Chivalry.* Worcester: Holl and Brandish, 1795.

Drane, Augusta T. *The Knights of St. John with the Battle of Lepanto and Siege of Vienna.* London: Burns and Lambert, 1858.

Faber, Frederick W. *Poems.* London: Richardson, 1856.

Fairholt, Frederick W. *Costume in England.* London: Chapman and Hall, 1846.

Favine, Andrew. *The Theatre of Honour and Knighthood.* London: Jaggard, 1623.

Fellows, Frank. 'Poems' in *Memoriam and Knights Hospitallers of St. John of Jerusalem.* London: Privately printed, 1890.

Fincham, Henry W. *The Order of the Hospital of St. John of Jerusalem and Its Grand Priory of England*. London: W. H. and L. Collingridge, 1915.

Fosbroke, Thomas. 'Rothley. The preceptory', *Transactions of the Leicestershire Archaeological and Historical Society* 12 (1922), 39–40.

Froude, James A. *The Spanish story of the Armada and Other Essays*. London: Longman and Green, 1892.

Gladstone, William. *Diaries,* ed. Henry C.G. Mathew. 17 vols. Oxford: OUP, 1994.

Godwin, George and John Britton. *The Churches of London*. London: Tilt, 1839.

Gough, Foster. *Narrative of the Knights Templars and Crusaders*. London: Bond, 1847.

Gough, Richard. *Sepulchral Monuments in Great Britain Applied to Illustrate the History of Families, Manners, Habits and Arts at the Different Periods from the Norman Conquest to the Seventeenth Century*. London: J. Nichols, 1786–96.

Hamilton Smith, Charles. *Selections of the Ancient Costume of Great Britain and Ireland from the 7th to the 16th Century Out of the Collection in the Possession of the Author*. London: Colnaghi, 1814.

Henty, George. *Knight of the White Cross*. London: Blackie, 1895/6.

Hodges, Michael. *Roll of deceased British Members of the order of Malta from the 19th century to 2018*. London: British Association, 2019.

Holbrook, Ann. *Constantine Castriot; An Historical Tale Taken from Authentic Documents of the Memorable Siege of Malta in the Year 1565*. Rugeley: J. Simpson, 1829.

Irving, George V. 'Knights templar in Scotland', *Notes and Queries* 3rd series 8 (1865), 312.

Keightley, Thomas. *Secret Societies of the Middle Ages*. London: Cox, 1846.

King, Edwin J. *The Pilgrimage of 1926. Being the Official Journal of the Order of St. John*. London, 1926.

———. *The Rules, Statutes and Customs of the Hospitallers, 1099–1310*. London: Methuen, 1934.

———. *The Knights of St. John in the British Realm*. London: 1934, revd. 1967.

Kingsley, Rose G. *The Order of St. John of Jerusalem Past and Present*. London: Skeffington, 1918.

Knight, Charles. *Penny Cyclopaedia of the Society for the Diffusion of Useful Knowledge*. London: Charles Knight, 1843.

———. *Old England: A Pictorial Museum of Regal, Ecclesiastical, Baronial, Municipal and Popular Antiquities*, 2 vols. London, 1845–6.

Larking, Lambert, ed. *The Knights Hospitaller in England*. London: Camden Society, 1857.

Maidment, James. Templaria. *Papers Relative to the History, Privileges and Possessions of the Scottish Knights Templar and Their Successors the Knights of St. John of Jerusalem*. Edinburgh: Cengage Gage, 1830.

Melville, Herman. *Apple Tree and Other Sketches,* ed. Henry Chapin. Princeton: University Press, 1922.

———. *Journal of a Visit to London and the Continent 1849–50*, ed. Eleanor M. Metcalf. London: Cohen and West, 1949.

———. *Journals,* ed. Howard C. Horsford and Lynn Horton. Chicago: Northwestern University Press, 1989.

Meyrick, Samuel. *A Critical Inquiry into Ancient Armour as It Existed in Europe But in Particular in England from the Norman Conquest to the Reign of Charles II, with a Glossary of Military Terms of the Middle Ages.* 3 vols. London: Robert Jennings, 1824.

Montagnac, Baron Elize. *Histoire des Chevaliers Hospitaliers de Sant-Jean de Jerusalem.* Paris: Auguste Aubry, 1863.

Morshead, John Y.A. *The Templars Trials.* London: Stevens and Sons, 1888.

O'Neal Haye, Anthony. *The Persecution of the Knights Templars.* Edinburgh: Constable, 1865.

Order of St. John of Jerusalem. *A Brief Notice of Its Foundation and Constitution and Its Objects in England.* London: St. John's Gate, 1878.

Piozzi, Hester and Penelope Pennington. *Intimate Letters 1788–1821,* ed. Oswald G. Knapp. London: John Lane, 1914.

Porter, Anna Maria. *The Knight of St. John.* London: Longman, 1817/8.

Porter, Whitworth. *A History of the Knights of Malta or the Order of St. John of Jerusalem.* London: Longman, Brown and Green, 1858.

Radcliffe, Ann. *Gaston de Blondeville.* London: Henry Colburn, 1833.

Saunders, Phyllis. *Within the Magic Gateways. A Fairy Tale of the Temple.* London: Harrap. 1919.

Scott, Walter. *Ivanhoe,* ed. Graham Tulloch. Edinburgh: Edinburgh University Press, 1997.

———. *The Siege of Malta and Bizarro,* ed. J.H. Alexander, Judy King and Graham Tulloch. Edinburgh: Edinburgh University Press, 2008.

———. *Introduction and Notes from the Magnum Opus. Ivanhoe to Castle Dangerous,* ed. J.H. Alexander, Peter Garside and Claire Lamont. Edinburgh: Edinburgh University Press, 2012.

Sermons preached at the 700th anniversary of the consecration of the Temple church. London: Macmillan, 1885.

Slous, Angiolo Robson. *The Templar: A Play in Five Acts and Verse.* London: Chapman and Hall, 1850.

Smirke, Sydney. *The Architecture, Embellishments and Painted Glass of the Temple Church.* London: John Weale, 1845.

St. John Hope, William. 'The Round Church of the Templars at Temple Bruer, Lincolnshire', *Archaeologia* 61 (1905), 177–98.

Taaffe, John. *The History of the Holy, Military, Sovereign Order of St. John of Jerusalem,* 4 vols. London: Hope and Co., 1852.

Tenison, Eva M. *Chivalry and the Wounded. The Knights of St. John of Jerusalem 1014–1914.* London: Gill, 1914.

Thackeray, William. *Notes of a Journey from Cornhill to Cairo by Way of Lisbon, Athens and Constantinople.* London: Chapman and Hall, 1846.

Till, W. *A Concise History of the Ancient and Illustrious Order of the Knights Hospitallers of St. John of Jerusalem, Rhodes and Malta; and of the Ancient Gate and Priory St. John's Square.* London: Effingham Wilson, 1834.

Torr, Cecil. *Rhodes in Modern Times.* Cambridge: CUP, 1887.

Walford, Weston S. 'On Cross-Legged Effigies Commonly Appropriated to the Templars', *Archaeological Journal* 1 (1845), 49–52.

Wallen, William. *The History and Antiquities of the Round Church at Little Maplestead, Essex.* London: John Weale, 1836.

Walpole, Horace. *Letters,* ed. Wilmarth S. Lewis, 37 vols. New Haven: Yale, 1937–83.

Werner, Zacharias. *The Brethren of the Cross,* trans. Elizabeth Lewis. London: G. Bell, 1882.

———. *The Templars in Cyprus,* trans. Elizabeth Lewis. London: Bohn, 1886.

Winthrop, William. 'The English, Irish and Scottish Knights of the Order of St. John of Jerusalem', *Notes and Queries* 7 (1853); 8 (1853), 99–101, 263–7, 333–4, 417; 442–4; 1854, 80–1.

Woodhouse, Frederick. *The Military Religious Orders of the Middle Ages: The Hospitallers, the Templars, the Teutonic Knights and Others.* London: S.P.C.K., 1879.

Woof, Richard. *Sketch of the Knights Templars and the Knights Hospitallers of St. John of Jerusalem with Notes on the Masonic Templars.* London: R E Taylor, 1865.

———. *A Brief Narrative of the Circumstances Attending the Revival and Progress of the English Langue of the Order of St. John of Jerusalem.* (unpublished) London, 1872.

Wright, Sydney Fowler. *Siege of Malta, Founded on an Unfinished Romance by Sir Walter Scott.* London: Tom Stacey, 1972.

Websites

www.nationaltrustcollections.org.uk
www.royalacademy.org.uk
http://godwindiary.bodleian.ox.ac.uk
www.open.ac.uk/Arts/reading>uk
www.rct.org.uk
museumstjohn.org.uk
www.rmg.co.uk
www.odnb.com
historicengland.org.uk
worcestermasonicmuseum.co.uk

Secondary: books and articles

Baker, John H., 'The Influence of Robert Southey's "the Origin of the Rose" on Robert Browning's "The Heretic's Tragedy"', *Westminster Research-Papers on Literary Studies* https://westminsterresearch.westminster.ac.uk.

Barber, Malcolm. *The New Knighthood. A History of the Order of the Temple.* Cambridge: CUP, 1994.

Bell, Barbara. "…Anything Like the Words": How Stage Performances from *Ivanhoe* Brought Scott's Characters to the Widest Audiences', *The Wensham Review of Literature and Culture* 13 (2) (2020), 69–97.

Brighton, Simon. *In Search of the Knights Templars.* London: Weidenfeld and Nicholson, 2008.

Cavaliero, Roderick. *The Last of the Crusaders.* London: Hollis and Carter, 1960.

Cox, Philip. *Novels and Verse Narratives on the Stage 1790–1840.* Manchester: University Press, 2000.

Demurger, Alain, 'The Knights Templar between Theatre and History: Raynouard's Works on the Templars'. *MO* 3 (1805–13), 45–52.

Ferguson, Robin. *The Knights Templar in Scotland.* Stroud: History Press, 2013.

Girouard, Mark. *The Return to Camelot.* New Haven: Yale, 1981.

Goldsworthy, Vesna. *Inventing Ruritania. The Imperialism of the Imagination.* New York: Columbia University Press, 2013.

Griffith-Jones, Robin and David Park eds. *The Temple Church in London. History, Architecture and Art.* Woodbridge: Boydell, 2017.

——— and Eric Fernie. *Tomb and Temple. Reimagining the Sacred Buildings of Jerusalem.* Woodbridge: Boydell, 2018.

Haag, Michael. *The Templars: History and Myth. From Solomon's Temple to the Freemasons.* London: Profile, 2008.

Hankin, Nigel. 'Acquiring Heritage: The Order of St. John and the Accumulation of Its Past (1858–1931)', in *Modern Memory* ed. Rory Maclellan. Abingdon: Routledge, 2022, 43–63.

Harris, Oliver. 'Antiquarian Attitudes: Crossed Legs and the Evolution of an Idea'. *The Antiquaries Journal,* 90 (2020), 401–40.

Horswell, Mike. *The Rise and Fall of British Crusader Medievalism, c. 1825–1945.* Abingdon: Routledge, 2016.

Hurlock, Kathryn. *Wales and the Crusades 1092–1291.* Cardiff: University of Wales Press, 2011.

Kenwood, Sydney H. 'The Influence of Lessing in England'. *Modern Language Review* 9 (1914), 344–58.

Kenworthy Browne, John. 'Plaster Casts from the Crystal Palace, Sydenham'. *Sculpture Journal* 15 (2006), 173–98.

Lewer, David and Robert Dark. *The Temple Church in London.* London: Historical Publications, 1997.

Lewis, Wilmarth S. *Horace Walpole's Library.* Cambridge: CUP, 2010.

MacLellan, Rory. *The Modern Memory of the Military-Religious Orders. Engaging the Crusades,* ed Rory Maclellan. Abingdon: Routledge, vol. 7. 2022.

Miele, Chris. 'Gothic Sign, Protestant Regalia: Templars, Ecclesiologists and the Round Churches at Cambridge and London'. *Architectural History* 53 (2010), 191–215.

Nicholson, Helen. *The Knights Templar.* London: Robinson, 2010.

O'Malley, Gregory. *The Knights Hospitaller of the English Langue 1460–1565.* Oxford: OUP, 2005.

Park, Judy H., 'The Limits of Empire in Davenant's the Siege of Rhodes'. *Mediterranean Studies* 24 (2016), 47–76.

Partner, Peter. *The Murdered Magicians. The Templars and Their Myth.* Oxford: OUP, 1987.

Rees, William. *The Order of St. John of Jerusalem in Wales and on the Welsh Border.* Cardiff: Western Mail and Echo, 1947.

Richard J. Schoek, 'The Elizabethan Society of Antiquaries and Men of Law'. *Notes and Queries* 199 (1954), 417–21.

Riley-Smith, Jonathan. *Hospitallers. The History of the Order of St. John.* London: Hambledon Press, 1999.

———. 'The Order of St. John in England, 1827–58'. *MO* 2 (2017), 121–42.

Siberry, Elizabeth. *The New Crusaders. Images of the Crusades in the 19th and Early 20th Centuries.* Aldershot: Ashgate, 2000.

———. 'Images and Perceptions of the Military Orders in Nineteenth Century Britain'. *Ordines Militares-Colloquia Torunensia Historica* 11 (2001), 197–209.

———. 'John Taaffe: Poet and Historian of the Order of St. John'. Forthcoming *MO* 8.

————. 'The Crusades: The Nineteenth Century Readers' Perspective'. *Perceptions of the Crusades in the Nineteenth and Twentieth Centuries.* Abingdon: Routledge, 2018.

————. *Tales of the Crusaders-Remembering the Crusades in Britain.* Abingdon: Routledge, 2021.

————. 'Variations on a Theme. Harry Pirie-Gordon and the Order of Sanctissima Sophia'. *MO* 7 (2019), 237–47.

————. 'Victorian Perceptions'. *MO* 1 (1994), 365–73.

Sultana, Donald. *The Siege of Malta Rediscovered. An Account of Sir Walter Scott's Mediterranean Journey and Last Novel.* Edinburgh: Scottish Academic Press, 1977.

Swarbrick, Lizzie. 'Templar Pseudo-History, Symbology and the Far Right', in *Modern Memory*, ed. Rory Maclellan. Abingdon: Routledge, 2022, 21–43.

Tennyson, Charles and Hope Dyson. *The Tennysons. Background to Genius.* London: Macmillan, 1974.

Thake, Robert. *A Publishing History of a Prohibited Best Seller: The Abbe Vertot and His Histoire de Malte.* Delaware: Oak Knoll Press, 2016.

Vann, Theresa. 'John Kaye, the "Dread Turk" and the Siege of Rhodes'. *MO* 3 (2017), 245–52.

———— and Donald J. Kagay, *Hospitaller Piety and Crusader Propaganda: Guillaume de Caoursin's Description of the Ottoman Siege of Rhodes 1480.* Aldershot: Ashgate, 2015.

Walker, John, 'From the Holy Grail and the Ark of the Covenant to Freemasonry and the Priory of Sion-An Introduction to the Afterlife of the Templars'. *MO* 5 (2012), 449–60.

————. 'The Templars Are Everywhere: An Examination of the Myths Behind Templar Survival after 1307' in *The Debate on the Trial of the Templars, 1307–14*, ed. Jochen Burgtorf, Paul. Crawford and Helen Nicholson. London: Routledge, 2016.

Webster, William. 'An Alternative to Ecclesiology: William Wallen (1807–53)'. *Ecclesiology Today* 42 (2010), 9–28.

Wood, Juliette, 'The Myth of Secret Society or It's Not Just the Templars Involved in Absolutely Everything'. *MO* 5 (2017), 449–60.

Zammit, William. 'Vertot's Histoire des Chevaliers de Malte. Its Prohibition in the Context of Hospitaller Historiographical Practices'. Entre Deus e Rei. O Mundo des Ordens Militares (2018), 107–36

Index

For Product Safety Concerns and Information please contact our EU
representative GPSR@taylorandfrancis.com
Taylor & Francis Verlag GmbH, Kaufingerstraße 24, 80331 München, Germany

www.ingramcontent.com/pod-product-compliance
Lightning Source LLC
Chambersburg PA
CBHW071748270326
41928CB00013B/2846

9 781032 011219